905

3

Growing Up Stupid Under the Union Jack

Also by Austin Clarke

Growing Up Stupid Under the Union Jack

a memoir
by Austin Clarke

McCLELLAND AND STEWART

To Sarah MacCulloch

Copyright © 1980 by Austin Clarke

The Canadian Publishers
McClelland and Stewart Limited
25 Hollinger Road, Toronto M4B 3G2

Canadian Cataloguing in Publication Data

Clarke, Austin C., date
  Growing up stupid under the Union Jack

ISBN 0-7710-2131-3

1. Clarke, Austin C., date — Biography — Youth.
2. Authors, Canadian (English) — Biography — Youth.*
I. Title.

PS8505.L36Z53 1980   C813'.54   C80-094123-3
PR9199.3.C54Z468

Printed and bound in Canada
by John Deyell Company

ONE

I was admitted to Combermere School, a secondary school in Barbados, on Roebuck Street, in Town, in September 1944, and placed in the "L2D," the Lower Second Form, with thirty other boys. For all these years, I have been wondering whether the "D" in L2D stood for "dunce." And nobody so far has told me.

But that was a day of personal rejoicing for my mother. She had at last achieved something beyond the expectations of the village. The village of St. Matthias rejoiced with her on that day. The poor and ambitious mothers gave me their blessing, and in their stern and frightening voices, they said, "Go 'long, boy, and *learn*! Learning going make you into a man."

And Delcina, the tallest, blackest and most beautiful woman I had ever seen, smiled and broke into a hymn. She lifted her operatic voice, trained in the hot broiling sun, as she bent over tubs of many sheets and shirts, with her black hands in the heavy soap suds, for the rich *out the front road*, and she sang on that morning. The washing, white as snow and ironed like glass, would be carried later in the week to the Marine Hotel.

Delcina sang a beautiful hymn that morning as I walked down the gap from my house on my way to a new but uncertain world. Delcina sang, *O God, Our Help in Ages Past*. My

5

book bag was filled with books of interminable pages, with puzzles of new knowledge undreamed of by my mother and by anybody else in the village. There was the shining gold-painted set that contained the compasses; the Rankin biscuit tin, scrubbed clean and looking like a small silver coffin, with a flying-fish sandwich in it; and my Ferrol bottle of "clear" lemonade, without the label on it.

On the previous Sunday, one of the "uncles" in that vicious circle of men, with a pair of scissors and a broken glass-bottle for a razor, had sat me down on the throne of a chair, under the clammy-cherry tree, and when I got up, my head was *clean*.

"Don't mind them few scratches and bumps I had to leave round the back of your head, boy. You is a Combermere boy now!"

The finished product had the impact and the look of a bowl on your head, and all the visible hair wiped clean away with soap and water by the blade of the glass-bottle. The smell of Limacol was strong even as I entered the large iron gate of Combermere School on that shaking, quivering morning, grabbed by the hand by my equally scared mother.

Combermere School was for middle- and lower middle-class boys. It was a second grade school. It would turn me into a civil servant, if I did well. If I didn't do well, it would turn me into a sanitary inspector. If I did even worse than that, into a "bookkeeper" on one of the many sugar plantations, to ride about on a horse in the sun, under a khaki helmet, dressed in a khaki suit, to drive some of my less fortunate friends and neighbours to work in the fields.

In those days the prospect of the sanitary inspector appealed more to me. I had seen them flitting about the village like black mosquitoes, a ladle in their hands, dipping into people's drinking water buckets and pigs' urinals, and pronouncing ruin and plague and pestilence at the sight of *larvees*; and having more drinks than doing work. That kind of drama and tragedy impressed me. I was at the beginning of having a choice in life.

But to be a civil servant, that was beyond my wildest dreams! Could I be like one of those powerful young men, walking up and down the corridor of the Old Public Buildings on the second and third floors, with huge important files of all colours — blue, red, white, faded and musty — dressed in white shirts and ties like the white Colonial officers who ruled and ran the country and who had the knack of looking important?

"Not on your blasted bottom dollar!" my mother said, imagining greater things. "I want you to be a *doctor*, hear?"

To be a doctor in those days, you had to know Latin backwards and forwards. You had to be a "Latin fool." *Amas, amat* and *amamus* would be the only things to save me from the hot sun of the bookkeeper; from the *larvees* of the sanitary inspector, dressed like a soldier of health; and from the low salary of the civil servant.

The other possibility was to be an elementary school teacher. But you had to have brains, and slightly more patience than brains if you wanted to be a school teacher; and you had to love children — and even more, lower wages. I was tempted by my own dreams to settle for the *amo amas amat*.

On that terrifying morning, ignorant of the meaning of higher education, and of Combermere School for Boys, and big books, and foreign languages of Latin and French, I waited in the hall with the other one hundred new boys, all of us stiff in our new khaki uniforms, clean heads, new ties of blue and gold which were the school colours, and which choked us; with our book bags made of blue denim, some of leather boasting the goodwill of a "relative" who lived Away, meaning most likely America. Our bags were filled with heavy books priced at more than most of our parents earned in a month. To those of us who did not win scholarships or receive government bursaries, the tuition fees were the devastating amount of eight dollars a term, which lasted

7

three months. But Combermere meant we were to be the new leaders of the country, and members of the Barbados middle class.

The headmaster was a Santa Claus of a man. A man of the cloth. He was bull-frogged and deep-voiced, but lovable as a cherub; a man who liked cricket, and who would take your ability to play it into consideration when you were sent to him for a flogging. The Reverend A. E. Armstrong, BA (Durham), MA (Someplace). In our unexplained tradition of giving almost every living person a nickname, he was known as "The Buff." We called him The Buff behind his back, naturally; and we tipped our caps in his white-suited presence and called him "Sir!"

During my first term, I never came within his Church-of-England presence; never sat at his feet, for he taught Scripture in the first form, and Latin in the higher forms; and I was in L2D. But at the end of that first year, before he left for retirement and England, I was "sent" to him for a flogging. I had to stand on the long wooden bench in front of his office. And while I waited for him, I wilted with uncertainty from the rumours about his strength and cruelty and dexterity with a tamarind rod. All the time, smaller boys, big boys, the school prefects and the master who had "sent" me paused and jeered and "skinned" their teeth at me, imitating the rod of The Buff's justice "in your arse!"

After one academic year, I was old enough and wise in the ways of the school to know that I should shriek with pain even before the first blow landed on my starched khaki trousers. For my offence — making a whistling sound with a mechanical pencil my friend Kenny had received from his mother in America — I could get three lashes.

But this was nothing like the flogging orgies I had witnessed and sometimes suffered through at my previous school, St. Matthias Boys' School. There the headmaster used the belt from a sewing machine. Rumour was that he soaked it in pee every night. And during the long hot afternoons he walked

8

throughout his empire of benches and blackboards and "desses," with the whip hanging around his neck like a dead black snake.

In comparison, the Reverend Armstrong, a man of great theological tolerance and knowledge, close to the altar and the communion cup, was a saint.

"Clarke!"

His voice was like large stones in a deep bucket. It was an authoritarian English voice. The water had already settled in my eyes. My body was waiting for the explosion of the rod. All I had to do now was scream so loud that the Reverend's understanding of Christian love and charity and pity would freeze his hand or lighten the blow; and he would say, "Dismiss, Clarke!"

"Bend over!" he said instead. The voice was still hoarse.
Wap!
"Go!"

And I left, laughing to myself the moment I was out of sight; eager again to dare the form master, and reassure the boys, "Man, The Buff can't lick, in truth! I didn't feel nothing. . . " And then to be welcomed back into the class as a hero, as a "bad boy."

One morning at St. Matthias the sun was already hot, although it was only nine o'clock. The perspiration was mixing with the coconut oil or the Brilliantine or vaseline which we wore on our hair. When I reached the school gate, and bolted to the entrance of the school, crossing the yard which had no grass, which never had any grass, and up the single step, when I reached the front door that morning, the headmaster was already there. Something had happened. Something was going

9

to happen. The entire school of two hundred boys were singing "Rock of Ages." They had reached the last verse. But the headmaster loved singing and loved that song. He delighted in leading the bass section among his teachers: tenors, altos and less profundo basses; and so the hymn had to be sung from the beginning again. He could sing a hymn or a song ten times.

I stood at the door. Five other boys who were late stood silently beside me. We were three minutes late. The headmaster accepted no excuses. Once a boy told him, "Please, sir, I had was to go 'cross the road five times to bring water for my mother and for the sheeps, 'cause my mother sick with badfeels." The headmaster listened carefully and patiently. In our hearts we cheered for the little boy. There could be no better excuse. But when the confession was over, the pee-soaked black snake was wrapped six times across the boy's back, like the Cross of St. Andrew. And when it was over, four of us had to carry the boy out like a casualty, to the pipe across the school yard, and wash the faeces from his legs and pants. We all swore then, as we stood under the pipe, in the frightened secrecy of our hearts, to soon become men, strong men, and come back for the headmaster with a bull-pistle whip.

This morning I stood at the door, facing the Union Jack. It was pinned against the wall below the grandfather clock, which the headmaster wound every morning with a key he kept in his pocket. Once he asked me to wind the clock, and I knew that something had happened to me, and certainly to him. The boys were now singing O God, Our Help in Ages Past. The voices were beautiful. Some of these voices belonged in the choir of the church which was separated from our school by a thick wall. It was made of stone and marl and lime and dust, and it covered our hands each time we jumped over it to steal the almonds which grew in the church yard. Now the school had become a church.

The hymn had come to an end. The school became very quiet. I could imagine the vicar walking up the aisle with the choir. It was still, like the hour before the school inspector was due to arrive and inspect our progress to send his report and our results back to England.

The headmaster wore white. He always wore white. He wore white as if it meant something which we boys could never aspire to; and he wore a tie that had no tropical colour in it. Around the knot he wore a pure, real, "true-true gold" ring, as the boys said. He walked like a tall black king, from the bottom of the one-room school right up to the platform. He held the bell, a dinner bell in size to the larger brown one which summoned the beginning of classes, and he touched its tongue with a finger.

But the school was already at attention. Nobody was breathing, including his teachers, who feared him as we trembled in his presence. From his side pocket he took a black object, something that looked like a huge hairpin. It was his tuning fork. He struck it against the desk, and it spoke the correct note and pitch he wanted. He hummed, "Do, re, me, faaaaaa!" In his youth he had won competitions for his voice. He struck the tuning fork again, and listened to its hum, and again he hummed, "Do, re, me, *faa*."

"*Ride on!*" he said, announcing the hymn. When he announced hymns and sang the first few lines, he was calm and loving and like a choir master. He loved singing hymns, and he transferred some of that love on to us.

But this morning he rushed from the platform and in three strides reached the door where we were standing. He became like a giant. So we galloped into the hymn *Ride on, ride on, in Majesty*, careful to let him know that we loved singing, and that we knew the words.

He was towering above us now. The long desk at the back was cleared of exercise books, nib pens, pencil boxes and boys. It looked clean, cleared away like a tribunal or a scaffold.

11

The entire school and the teachers were singing at the top of their voices.

Ride on, ride on, in Majesty!
In lowly pomp ride on to die. . .

"Fingers!" he said to the six of us at the door.

The boy at the head of the line held out his hands. The headmaster inspected his fingers and nails. They were dirty. They were always dirty. We always had dirty fingernails. Not one of us in that school had ever held a nail file in our hands. They were not common in our village. When the time came, we cleaned our fingers with a stick.

We pitched marbles morning, noon and night, and our nails bore that evidence. He knew they were dirty; he knew they would always be dirty; that not one of the six of us in the late line would remember to use the stick. We seemed to want the inspection and the punishment.

He held the boy's ear and looked inside it, and then the other. Then he pushed him gently aside, like an approved piece of merchandise. And he inspected the rest of us, and pushed us aside. We were now thinking of the brimstone and ashes of his fierce temperament. And in all this time, the school was singing, like a choir of a cathedral, at the top of their voices.

Ride on, ride on, in Majesty!
The last and fiercest strife is nigh. . .

He threw the black snake across the neck of the boy nearest him. Then he was flogging all six of us at the same time, across our backs, our heads, our feet as we jumped in stupid attempts to avoid the snake, criss-crossing, horizontal, diagonal, like the various crosses in the English flag and in the flags of other countries he had taught us about in classes of social history. We smelled his chalk. We smelled his breath.

12

And we could hear from that close, chilling distance the deep profundo of his voice, for as he flogged us he was singing along with the teachers and the rest of the school, singing and flogging with the pre-soaked, pee-soaked fan belt from his wife's sewing machine.

> *Look down with sad and wondering eyes*
> *To see the approaching Sacrifice.*

And when it was over, when we had come galloping and exhausted and *whemmed* to the end of the hymn, and he was perspiring, his black skin jewelled with beads, he touched the tongue of the dinner bell and silence reigned.

TWO

Beyond us, in the meantime, the Second World War was raging on the high seas and on battlefields in strange countries. In the magazines which trickled through the blockades of ships and reached us, in the pages of *Life* and *English Country Life*, *Punch* and *Reader's Digest*, we would see the war in pictures. We would see American GI's, stronger than Charles Atlas, drinking cans of grapefruit juice and overturning German tanks with their bronzed bare hands. We all wanted either to be Americans or else to live in America. So we lived through the defeats and victories of the British Empire and her Allies. We praised Churchill for a time, and thought of praising Stalin too. We hated Hitler and Mussolini, as if we were on the Field of Flanders. The church wall meanwhile was painted with the swastikas of our irrepressible graffiti.

The headmaster cleared his throat. He was about to make an important announcement. It was a speech of sorrow. The Germans had sunk another merchant ship. The headmaster called the ship by name, and he read off the names of the dead at sea. Some were men who had walked about our streets a few months before, unemployed and barefooted, whistling the last hit tunes; men whom we had remembered passing us along streets that had no paving, no macadam, streets which kicked up the dust of these men's former cocky independence. These men were now names on a folded news-paper page.

Men from our village and from neighbouring villages had gone to sea, not to fight the Germans whom they did not know, not to die for the Empire, as the headmaster told us in his stern, sad voice, but as we knew, they had ventured forth because we were to be the beneficiaries of their hard, swirling seafaring labour. They left to make a living. Unemployment or "no work," as we called it in our village, was as prevalent as the dust in the public road.

For three silent minutes we stood in respect for the dead of our village "lost at sea." Our eyes filled with tears at the unfairness of it all, and at the frightening images of men falling out of ships, in seas higher than the crown of the clock in the tower of the Garrison Savannah, higher than any building in our island-country, higher than any wave we had seen off the Gravesend Beach, and blacker too.

He told us it was in the Atlantic Ocean that it happened. He told us about the Atlantic all over again, and called it "one of the biggest bodies o' salt water, boys." The men, who on the other occasions when he enlightened us on the darkness of our history, men who had discovered us, those same men, he told us now, had crossed this very Atlantic Ocean hundreds of years and miles before. And now the Germans were ruling these same waters and waves, and killing fathers, brothers and uncles from our village. And as black Britons we wanted to do something about it.

That sad morning the headmaster said a very long prayer. We prayed for the King and the Royal Family, and the Prime Minister of England, and for all our Allies; with closed eyes and lowered heads, we asked God to give our English leaders good counsel, wisdom and strength to kill more Germans and Italians and Japanese than the Axis Powers could do to us "in these days of peril." The headmaster read from the *Book of Common Prayer*, something about us *calling out of the depth of misery, and out of the jaws of death, which is ready now to swallow us up. . .* And I got very scared and was glad it was not night. Then he said something about our sins and about our *sins now crying out against us for vengeance; but hear us thy poor servants begging mercy, and imploring thy help, and that thou wouldest be a defence unto us against the face of the enemy.* We knew he meant the Germans and the "Axes" were our enemies. He had taught us that much patriotism.

The headmaster brought the sad proceedings to a close by leading us into the singing of *Rule Britannia, Britannia Rule the Waves.* And in all the singing, nobody remembered to pray for the families of the Barbadian seamen lost or dead at sea.

Combermere School could never match the drama of learning and instruction that was staged daily at St. Matthias Boys' School. At Combermere, a new school at this time, with two storeys and a corridor on both floors which we used to practise the hundred-yard dash, at this school we sat at individual *desses* and marked our initials "on the desses of time," as one bright boy said; and gouged secret coded declarations of love for girls.

Inside our desses we kept our almost unaffordable books, along with our lunch. And when the last bell rang at three in the afternoon, we secured these possessions with a padlock and kept the key tied to a long piece of string and showed it proudly on a school bus or in the street, arrogant in this display because we were "Cawmere boys."

At Combermere I learned about the two sides of an

isosceles triangle; was told that x was equal to 2 and y to 3, if certain things happened; and was left alone in fear to figure out the value of z. We were taught the capitals of almost every known country in the British Empire; *amo, amas, amat*; *je suis, tu suis, il suit*; about the birth and life of Christ in the Gospels; and I learned how to pronounce "pseudonym."

The way the master taught Scripture at Combermere was nothing like the way Miss Smith taught it in Sunday School. Miss Smith was a young, round-faced woman in her twenties when I was eight or nine or ten. All of us Sunday School boys fell in love with her. We married her many times before she knew; and some brave boys who had heard of "woman things" beyond the reach of my tender carnal knowledge, or had read about it in magazines or in the underlined passages about David and Bathsheba in the Bible, they talked about taking Miss Smith to bed. They would then tell me with dramatic details bigger than their imagination what it was all about.

But Miss Smith made the Scriptures live. On Sunday evenings we went to bed with our minds made up to be "good little boys" or else filled with the damnation and everlasting darkness that was the lot of Lot or Goliath. The hell of her voice and of her threats was even blacker than the pictures she painted of hell and sinners.

One boy, impressed by the moral of David's disadvantage before Goliath, challenged the village bully to a fight. As a result, he did not attend Sunday School for the next three weeks while the swelling on the left side of his face, where Goliath's blow had landed, went down gradually, to again disclose an eye whose safety he had lost sight of.

The master at Combermere enters the classroom. He sits at his elevated dess, below the large blackboard nailed into the wall. And he opens his book to the lesson.

"What's the lesson for today?" he asks.

The monitor stands and says, "*Axe*, chapter one, sir?"

The previous time he had told us to study chapter one in the *Acts of the Apostles*; but this is the way they do things at the "big schools."

He would then ask each one of us, sitting in the order of the alphabet or in the order of our academic achievement, to recite a line; or if he was in a bad mood, two, three, four sentences.

Even the way he is dressed and the clothes he wears seem strange to me. At the elementary school the teachers (they were not called "masters") wore long-sleeved shirts and ties, and baggy long trousers. Their shirts were sometimes discoloured and "high" from sweating. And at the end of the day when they put on their jackets and jumped on their bicycles, the perspiration could be seen on their jackets too, for it had eaten through the underarms. But these were brave, honest men who studied hard at night and put themselves on a higher plane of learning, and acquired, after many years, external degrees from the University of London. They were beautiful black men.

At Combermere the masters (they were not "teachers") wore khaki shorts and clean white sweet-smelling shirts. Some of them wore suits.

In this class now we are seated in alphabetical order.

The master points a finger, as if he is too tired; points with a glaring eye and nods at the first boy in the first row of scared boys.

"Armstrong," he says and smiles.

We become tense as he smiles.

Armstrong stands up between his chair and dess, made of wood by the school carpenter. The room is quiet — like those mornings at St. Matthias when a flogging was in the air.

"Begin!" the master says.

Armstrong tries to look wise. And when that fails, he relaxes and looks stupidly at the ceiling.

Bright students at our school would always look up at the ceiling before answering a question. They would close their eyes once or twice to make the question seem more difficult. No one wanted to be known for answering easy questions.

"The former treatise have I made. . . " Armstrong says.

"Next boy, go on!"

Armstrong, E. E., who came after Armstrong, A. E., stands up.

"Spell treatise, EE!"

EE spells treatise. EE is bright.

"Next boy!"

And Babb stands up and says, ". . . O, Theophilus, of all that Jesus began to teach and do."

The master loses his temper and bellows, "Next idiot!"

Something is wrong. He says, "Next! Next idiot!" as each boy jumps up and tries to figure out what is wrong with Babb's answer.

Then all of a sudden a genius among us who has remembered the lesson by heart sees the point. He raises his hand in the air. He cannot speak before he is given permission to do so. In a weak, uncertain voice he says, ". . . both to do and teach."

"Yesss!" the master hisses. He smiles. Somebody in his class has an eye for detail, even if it is useless detail. He is gratified. "Come up above the asses!"

The smiling little genius, now hated by all of us, takes the seat of the other boys who missed the point in the question. After shuffling and snickering and threats under the breath for this little genius, the room becomes quiet again and the master offers to "enlighten our darkness."

"The important word in the first sentence of the *Axe*," he says, "is *both*. *Both* show you that there is two things involved here. The doing *and* the teaching. Jesus wanted his disciples to walk 'bout the place teaching, not like some of the reverends we have running 'bout this place but like real social workers."

The master was doing an external degree in sociology by correspondence from Wolsey Hall College. By the end of our first term, we learned that this master who taught us Scripture was an atheist and a communist.

"That is what studying all them big books on sociology does do to a man's brain," the little genius enlightened our darkness.

Apart from Scripture, we learned the declensions of Latin nouns and the first conjugation of Latin verbs. But we had more fun inventing our own Latin verbs.

We soon covered *amabo, amabis, amabit, amabitis, amabamus, amabunt*.

And the little genius, who was fast becoming an atheist himself and who borrowed *Das Kapital* from the public library, introduced us to the new Latin verb, *mary-hairy-co, mary-hairy-cit, mary-hairy-citis, mary-hairy-camus, mary-hairy-cunt!*

"What is the longest word in the *whirl*?"

"Mississippi."

"Spell it!"

"Who is the oldest man in the Bible?"

"Nicodemus?"

"No, he is the fellow who walk by night!"

"Who is the King of Englund?"

20

"George the Six', man! Everybody know that!"

"Betcha can't tell me how the King wee-wees when he's on parade shaking hands and inspecting the Guards!"

"I have a' uncle who uses to live in Amurca, and from there he went to live in Englund, and he tell me that the King have this thing, like a long piece o' rubber, yuh know? Tie on to the King's waist, just below the King shoe, and when the King want to wee-wee or fire a shit, all the King got to do is . . . that is the meaning of a King, to be a King."

And we laughed and learned and pitched marbles in the soft ground, and ran races on the playing field larger than we had ever played on; and we played cricket and football, and went home drowned in perspiration but proud "Cawmere boys" wearing the school tie slightly loosened because that was the style.

THREE

I remember that Christmas. It came soon after the end of the first term. I had passed the Michaelmas Examinations. I was now a high school boy, for I had passed my first exams. I was a choirboy too. I was moving up in the world, my mother concluded.

"Take off my clothes, please!" she commanded the moment I reached home from Combermere. "Take off my clothes and put on your home clothes."

My home clothes were those not good enough to be worn to church or school or Town, or to visit my countless uncles and aunts who lived in the country in St. James; or to be worn to the Empire Theatre on Saturday afternoons, where we met to see American movies and eat parched peanuts, "a penny a big bag, look muh here! You want me, young fellow?"

"You got your work to do. Don't play no sport with me this evening, boy!" my mother said. "You not at Cawmere now!"

Latin and French and the ability to spell the longest word in the whirl did not change my status in her eyes, in her book. The village had its rituals and customs, and these swallowed me up again the moment I entered its precincts. It was as if I was a laneway or a path or a "cane-brek," swallowed up and hidden after the rains by the strangulating vines and weeds and wild flowers that grew everywhere.

Christmas meant work. I never knew it to be only a religious festival. All our old furniture had to be scraped and painted or varnished. The house had to be cleaned from top to bottom. And since we did not sleep on factory-made mattresses, I had to cut fresh Guinea-grass and cush-cush grass. Sometimes I stole it or begged for it. I would bring it home in the hot sun and my neck would burn and scratch for days. I laid it out in the back yard for the sun to dry it out, to turn it from green into make-shift down.

Christmas also meant lots of food and torture. Shoes were deliberately bought too small. And my mother made me spend the two weeks before Christmas walking on old newspapers in the golden light of the kerosene lamp, "to stretch" the shoes to my size.

She kept me sitting up with her beyond the nodding time, my neck heavy from exhaustion, while she taught me how to make cushions from pieces of cloth she got from the village dressmaker and leftovers from the silk dress lengths she bought from the Indian man. Or we would make artificial flowers — roses out of crepe paper of pink and red and yellow and green and mauve. The only roses I saw like those in the school garden at St. Matthias were red. And I would smell these red roses all along the dark, close road to my house.

Always on these nights before Christmas, when the house was filled with women (there were few men around), they would tell stories of the war and of previous wars, of the village, of the volcanic dust that came from St. Vincent and covered the land and made the fowls jump on their *rooses* before it was midday; and stories of village boys who were "good" and who were "bad" and who were "too mannish"; of girls who got "in trouble" and boys who got girls "in trouble."

The stories they liked to tell most were about boys who supported their parents. No one ever talked about the fathers. Only after they were dead.

23

And the night would sometimes be filled with ghosts from stories, and the long-taled imaginations of these women, who knew women who worked "obeah" on men to get them to marry them or to turn them doatish after that first "dose of obeah didn' work, child"; stories of superstition and monsters and men with three heads. Stories of a "steel donkey," of "the sinner-men" and of a man who had no head and came out only at night. Once they told a story about a train which ran in Barbados, but I fell asleep before I could hear the end.

I would be sitting frozen with the sleep in my body, with the scissors in my hand, and my mother would catch me idle and say, as if her love had itself been napping, say so kindly in her soft voice, "Boy, why you don't turn in and get some sleep?"

And my sleep would be torment. I would writhe in terrors greater than those which chilled me from the Bible stories of sinners which Miss Smith told like Judy Garland. I would run on the unmoving bed of cush-cush grass and voicelessly call out for help from the clutches of a nightmare of white horses trampling me; and in the middle of that arthritis of limbs and voice, hear my mother calling out over the front window to the fisherwoman to buy flying fish "all-a-penny."

At this graveyard hour but no later than ten o'clock, still to my small mind an hour of cobwebs and ghosts, the fish tasted better than during the day. My mother would buy as many as she could clean. She boned them and washed them in lime juice, and seasoned them and floured them, and fried them over a fire made of dried sugar-cane roots. In good times the fire was stimulated and made more ferocious by the seeds of the mahogany tree.

"Come, boy, get up and run 'cross the road for a fresh bucket o' water for me. You sleeping?" She was terrified of the dark.

The dark road never had street lamps but always people bright with talk — perhaps a man and woman hiding beneath a window to steal a kiss — who kept me company along the

24

somnambulating fifty yards to the public stand pipe, the galvanized bucket heavy in my hand.

I would return to the nightmares and the riding horses and then, in the middle of peace and good "wet dreams," be awakened from the soaked bed mistaken for the school yard where we played, to be given six crispy fried flying fish, golden brown and hot with pepper.

"Nobody in this whirl should ever go to sleep hungry, boy," my mother always told me.

In the morning it would be time enough to surrender my cush-cush mattress to the sun to dry. If my mother woke up "on the wrong side," I would surrender my body for a flogging, for wetting-up the bed. "You too old to be always pissing-up your bed!"

But the smells of Christmas! The new paint and varnish and the golden apples and the sugar apples and mammy apples; the ham which had come wrapped in tar paper and had to be soaked in water for days before it was boiled; the great cake, soaked in rum since Easter; and the currants and raisins themselves soaked in rum along with the boiled peelings of grapefruit and orange; the coconut bread and the sponges. The puddings were made with more eggs than I had seen our hens laying, mixed by hand in one long night and done in one day of baking: mixing the butter from Australia, rancid as the sheep of the pampas that I would learn about in my geography classes. The freshly made artificial flowers and the Christmas dinner of roast pork with a crackling of dark-brown flavoured skin, which you chewed in a boastful "chaw" as if it were chewing gum, for hours after the meal, while walking through the lanes of the village. And rice and peas and doved peas and a thick porridge-like dish called "jug," something my mother told me had come with her from Africa. And sweet potatoes and tomatoes and rivers of sorrel, and one lip-wetting taste of rum, because "I don't want you to be growing up liking rum, you hear me?"

We ate in silent, jaw-moving seriousness because the rule in

25

our house said you "don't talk whilst you have food in your mouth." At the end I would literally have to be rolled on the floor, and my mother would rub down my belly with coconut oil. That was the way we ate on Christmas Day. I had eaten as if it were my last meal on earth.

My friends, Briggs, Mickey, George-Ben and Johnny, lived nearby. We would compare foods and presents, and plan to meet early on Boxing Day to run races.

"Wha' you get for Christmas?"

"Man, I ain't get nothing this time. My uncle in Amurca didn't send the letter."

"My mother give me a' apple. It come from Canada. It was wrap in a piece of paper that come from Canada too. She pay a shilling for it in Town. I keeping it till Old Year's Day before I eat it."

"You not going eat it till then?"

"You is a fool? Nobody don't eat a Canadian apple the same day. My mother say yuh have to watch it for a few days."

"Tomorrow is races."

"I'm going to be a jockey."

"I is a horse!"

"Man, you can't be a horse because you not fast enough. You have to be a jockey!"

The war was on. I do not remember getting presents wrapped in pretty paper at Christmas. But after the war there were other "wars" of money, of drought, of unemployment. Presents were never put under a tree. We never had Christmas trees. And snow never fell, so there were no white Christmases. But we all loved Bing Crosby and tried to sing like him. We dreamed and sang, sang and dreamed, but never saw a white Christmas.

We had all heard of a man named Father Christmas, and Miss Smith said he brought presents for boys and girls who were good. I was therefore not in that choir of angels. But we had balloons and red bells made of crepe paper, which opened in frills and were pinned in the rafters where there were cobwebs my mother could not reach with her broom.

On Christmas Day it was my job to get the "snow" to put around the house. This "snow" came from the rock quarry in the village. I would scrape up the whitest, prettiest marl and put it in the back yard, and keep it secret until four o'clock Christmas morning. Then I would spread it around the house, leading up to the single step made of limestone which stood like a white sentry.

The bells of the church began to ring half an hour before five o'clock on Christmas morning, when there were stars in Bethlehem and Barbados. It was the time to test one's Christianity, one's charity, one's finery, one's success in getting the new clothes on time, "home-made" by the free-wheeling dressmakers and tailors who sprang up like weeds. Every piece of clothing worn to church on Christmas morning had to be brand-new.

After church we caught the bus and went into town, and walked amidst the multitude of people to Queen's Park to listen to the Police Band under the direction of Captain Raison, an Englishman. He was the best-liked man in the country on Christmas morning. He had turned military musicians of the Police Band into a band playing calypsoes and Christmas carols with a beat. We would walk through the park and show off our new tailored jackets and short pants, and shirts made by aunts, bigger sisters and dressmakers who sometimes, in the rush of things, mistook our measurements for our sisters' and made us blouses instead.

We would walk soft and in pain from our new shiny, cheap John White shoes which had "English Made" printed at the sweaty, bladdered sides. If you were a high school boy, you took pains and bore the pain of your shoes, made sure to be visible and conspicuous, creaking up and down with fresh bladders on your feet, and eating "cocks" and "comforts" and "sweeties" and black sugar cakes and white sugar cakes and red sugar cakes and rolly-pollies, made by the local confectioners, the selling women who looked like birds of paradise on this bright God-spelling morning. "Comforts, toffees, pack o' nuts! Look muh here! Who calling? You want me, young fellow?" Their voices were like the breath of love on Christmas morning in the park.

I would meet my girl on this Christmas morning and walk her off to a side, away from the throbbing bass drum in the Police Band playing "Good King Wenceslaus" as if it were a fox trot, near the pens where the Agricultural Society kept birds and rabbits that were grown, for taunts and gifts of peanuts from children and from women in love. And I would tell her, my heart brimful with new love:

"Roses are red
Violets are blue. . . "

She would smile and blush, and touch the frills of her new white frock, and laugh and chew the fresh roasted peanuts I had bought out of my savings, one bright shilling with a King's head on it, my pocket money on Christmas Day.

FOUR

Our parents did not allow us to go to horse racing on the Garrison Pasture. It was for "big people": adults and crooks and women who "picked fares" and for pimps.

The Garrison Pasture was also known as a place where men and women did "things" at night, when the moon wasn't shining.

Fruits and "sweets" and bets were sold; and there was gambling under make-shift tents: cards and dice and cursing. There was never a Race Day that didn't end in bloodshed and tottering men who had lost their way home, from the kick of the "steam" and the "darrou" they had drunk from too many bottles.

"Man, fire one!"

"Gimme the kiss-me-arse snap-glass and let me show yuh I can fire one with yuh, man!"

And all these people congregated in the middle of the pasture, with the horses running around them. They betted on games of chance, trying to find the Ace of Spades or one polished seed under a tot.

Sometimes they raised their heads from their fortunes, when a race was being run. Once a boy was trampled by a horse, and the entire congregation of people cried and said, "Oh Jesus Christ, the horse kill-he dead, dead, dead, be-Jesus Christ!" And when the next race started, they forgot the boy.

But our races, the races we boys organized in our village, were better. The girls made the silks for the jockeys, and the boys made the whips. The whips were made from the spines of the palm leaf and woven together by cord. The cord was dyed in many colours. At the end of our whips we always had a piece of rubber. We called it the tongue. The colours for our whips — like the colours for our kites which came out around Easter, like harmless birds of prey, angry only at the trees and the telephone wires — were made from the juice of the berry of the spinach vine and from soaking coloured paper in water.

The fastest boys were the "horses." A piece of strong string was tied around the waist, as the reins. Our race course was the distance around the main building of the girls' school. No girl was allowed to be a jockey or a "horse." We did not play with girls on our village race day.

We held derbies of ten or more "horses" with their jockeys running behind them at break-neck speed, and *brek-toe* speed, at full gallop around the rock-infested schoolhouse. The jockeys wore their caps with the peaks turned up because they thought it made them look like the real jockeys on the Garrison. Their silks were ordinary shirts, too big, pulled out from the waist so they would billow in the wind. They were splashed with stripes and crosses and sashes made of bright colours.

The "horses" and jockeys stood at the tape, stomping the ground, foaming at the mouth, ready to tear around the school. The jockeys shouted, "Now, sir! Now, sir!" And some "horses" who forgot they were "horses" disagreed and shouted, "Not yet, sir! Not yet, sir!" because their trousers were falling down or they saw a large rock planted savagely in the ground over which they had to run. After each race these rocks took toll and nails out of our big toes. There would be toes with broken nails and with no nails at all, and some with big pieces of flesh ripped out of them.

FIVE

Combermere was far from my mind these days. I went to the beach with the boys and sat in the sun all day, pretending to be a fisherman. We caught crabs and dived for sea eggs, and picked welts and "sea beefs" off the reefs and the black slimy pipe that ran for miles, it seemed, from the shore far out, far on its way to America and England.

Canada was not talked about: it existed only in apples. It was a blur on our consciousness.

The pipe was filled with the sewage of the town and the hotels and the white people's homes. We would stand on this pipe and fall off, and pretend we were drowning, and shout, "Help, help! Helpppp!" and watch the men and the bigger boys come, like fish through the rough life-saving waves, doing the crawl. And then we would dive from their view and come up again, like a silent submarine, to emerge on the spluttering beach, catching our breath, laughing and jeering and bragging, "Man, I can swim like a shark! Drown, wha'?"

Once the cockiest among us bragged, "Man, I could swim like a shark and a half!" He drowned the first week of the next vacation. And we buried him in the graveyard of the church beside the school. None of us went to the beach that vacation.

"Once upon a time, and a very long time, there was a boy who uses to go up the hill every evening. And when all the people in the village was cooking and eating their food, and just before the sun went down behind the sea, this boy would shout out, 'Wolf! Wolf!' And the people would run and leave their food, and run up the hill to rescue the boy. And the boy would laugh and say, 'How there could be a wolf? You ever hear of wolves in Barbados?' And the men and women would go back down the hill.

"And the next evening the boy would go up the hill to get his sheep, and when the sun went down he would shout out, 'Wolf! Wolf!' and the people would leave their food and run up the hill, and he would laugh and tell them no wolves ever lived in Barbados, and the people would go back down the hill.

"And this went on for days and days. And one day when the sun did just gone down behind the sea and the sky look dark, the boy screel out, 'Wolf! Wolf! A real wolf!' And the people went on eating their food and saying, 'That boy does really make we laugh. He going grow up to be a good comedian one o' these days! Wolves in Barbados? He tell we so himself, more than one time, there ain't no wolves here. But that boy have a future as a comedian.'

"And the next morning, when the men and women went up the hill to tie out their sheep and goats, they saw an Alsatian dog eating out the boy's guts. 'But I won't call this a wolf! You would call this a wolf?' I step 'pon the wire, and the wire won't bend, and that's the way my story end!"

SIX

Everyone in the village — our mothers, big sisters, aunts, uncles and fathers — worked at some time at the Marine Hotel. It was a huge building washed in pink, with tall casuarina trees for miles and miles up in the blue sky; and at night it almost touched the stars which we counted beyond five hundred, although the sages of little boys among us said, "If you ever count past five hundred stars, yuh going *drop-down* dead, yuh!"

After midnight only ghosts and fowl-cock thieves walked the streets from the Marine, past the church which had a graveyard of dead Englishmen and English vicars and an English sailor which a tombstone called an "ensign."

And when we ventured too close to the walls of the Marine Hotel on Old Year's Night — the highest moment in our lives — the watchman, dressed in an old black jacket to suit the night, and khaki trousers rolled up above the ankles, and who knew the lay and geography of each rock and glass-bottle in the roads and lanes surrounding the grounds, this night watchman would challenge us. "Where the arse wunnuh think wunnuh going?"

If we stood our ground, which we never did, and stated our mission, which he never accepted, we would end up running from him, with the fear of his bull-pistle in our back.

We soon learned that we could take liberties only when he had a woman in the flower bed of blooming begonias.

On Old Year's Night there would be balloons with faces painted on them, bigger and prettier than we had ever seen before. And music by the best dance bands in the country. Coe Alleyne's Orchestra, Percy Greene's Orchestra and others. The music would slip over the wall which was too high and treacherous for us to climb.

Outside the free wall hundreds of boys and unemployed men, and some girls who were old enough to have boy-friends and be out at night, would stand in the dew dressed in men's jackets, always black, to keep the dew from seeping into our bones, so the old people said, and to give us consumption, which was our term for tuberculosis. We would dance to the music in our native rhythmic steps, moving over the pebbles in the road, and watch the white people inside because the Marine was "blasted serrigated."

The men inside wore formal black suits that turned them into undertakers. And the women were white in long dresses skating over the huge dance floor, slippery and dangerous to unpractised steps from the waxing which the watchman had given it the day before. "Woe betide the man who don't know a waltz from a trot when he step 'pon that floor!" he would boast to us.

We watched them from below the wall. And we dreamed of becoming powerful and rich, to join them, to be like them. The waiters, our "relatives," our family, were mingling among them now: our fathers, uncles and older brothers. And if we were looking at the right moment, we would see a wink cast in our direction, and in the wink the promise of a turkey leg, or a rum for the older boys. Perhaps a funny hat or a balloon that was not trampled at the stroke of midnight.

Once one of them, braver than the watchman, and smarter, sneaked a leg of turkey out to us before the ball was over. And we chomped on the cold strange-tasting meat all the way through "The Blue Danube," all the while making mincemeat with prettier steps than those trudging ladies and drunken gentlemen on the grand ballroom floor.

Five minutes before midnight it would become very quiet. Quiet like my old school down the gap fifty yards away, silent and asleep at this time of grave-digging darkness. The watchman would stand at attention. And when he knew that we had all seen him, he would walk through the midst of us like a general, like a plantation overseer; come right up to each one of us, twirling his stick right in our faces, like the drum major in the Volunteer Force, and say, "Don't mek no noise in front of the white people, you hear me?"

Four minutes before midnight. And we can see the *musicianers* with their instruments at the ready, and the ladies and gentlemen in the grand ballroom skipping here and there, looking for husbands or partners. And the lights would go off one by one, and suddenly the place would be like a fairy garden with only coloured bulbs, and the balloons like beads of sea water on the skin. And then the counting in a collection of voices, ours and theirs inside. "Twelve . . . eleven . . . ten . . . nine. . . ."

All of us outside counting in a year that would bring us more war, and nothing like what it would bring the ladies and gentlemen on the other side of the wall.

The counting growing louder now. ". . . five . . . four. . ." And we continue to ignore the watchman, whom we had long ago nicknamed "Hitler." And suddenly he too joins in the counting.

And then, on the stroke of midnight, the eruption of motorcar horns blowing, balloons popping; the waiting taxicabs honking, with a hint of deliberate impatience; and the ringing of bells, dinner bells and church bells; and the bursting of balloons, and the scuffling and fighting for the balloons thrown over the wall and floating in our direction; and the good fortune of a funny hat which has landed in our midst, barely destroyed, which we patched and for days afterwards wore as a statement: "Man, you went to the Marine Old Year's Ball? I went, man. I got this hat. Look!" Or a noise-maker sneaked out from behind the wall by a maid or a mother; and the boiled unsalted rice carried in paperbags; "them tourisses is people who suffer from sugar in the blood!"

We would walk back, happy, to our district, memorizing the night of magic and revelry and choruses and words of the most popular tune played by the Percy Greene Orchestra. *Goodnight, Irene* . . .

"Percy blow that tenor sax like po'try, boy! You hear how he take them riffs in the first chorus? Pure po'try, boy!"

"Day in and day out I working my fingers to the bone in that blasted Marine, and I can't see myself getting nowhere for it. It's slavery. Tomorrow is Monday, however, and the tourisses leffing. They going back up to Englund and Amurca. So the hotel laying off maids and butlers left and right. You need school newniforms. You need new school books. This Caw-mere costing me a fortune in new books. I wonder where next term school fees coming from. If my sister in Panama don't send the little thing, boy, you *loss*. You seen the post-man pass here recently? He pass for the week yet? This Christmas you shouldda hear the amount o' money the people say the postmens thief and take. There ain't no money coming in this place, so I don't see how they could accuse the poor postmens, though. But it ain't no wonder if they thief, 'cause the guvment pays them peanuts. Where am I going to get your school fees from this term, boy? Look! Come and write a letter to your aunt and find out what happen to the money order she promise to send. . . . "

My mother sat at my elbow. I would smell the honour and the sweat of her hard labour. To write or read was beyond the expectations the village held out to her. Certain passages of the Bible she had probably learned by heart — so often had she heard them read at St. Matthias Girls' School years before I was born. But she was careful that what she dictated to me to write down was just what she said and nothing more. She followed each turn and twist of the common pen. Some marvellous instinct told her when I had completed a word or when I ought to have done so.

The kerosene lamp was placed in the middle of the table. And she would squint her large beautiful eyes, just as we squinted ours at Combermere when we faced a difficult Latin word. The Bible was nearby. The Bible was always at hand. It was the only book, apart from my school books, that was our library. It was the only book I ever saw her look into: she would open the pages, turn her eyes up, and soon afterwards fall asleep. The hieroglyphics of the printed word induced an opiate of slumber and weakness of the eyes. "Learn, learn," she always told me. "You must learn, son. You hear me? Learn. Learning is next to godliness."

The writing paper was fine, English-made, and suitable for air mail correspondence. (We never wrote a local letter: we would walk with that message, or give it verbally to a friend, to give to a friend, to give to the person. I never could understand why.)

The bottle of Quink ink was English-made. The pen nib

was ready to be dipped into the rich majestic blue liquid, and I was ready to begin. . .

"Yuh didn't forget the day o' the mont', eh, son?" She pronounced it day-de-munt. "And write pretty like how Mr. Thorpe at St. Matthias teach you." She then dictated the salutation:

"My dear Aunt Eloise, I hope that the reaches of these few lines will find you in a perfect state of good health, as they leave me feeling fairly well at present."

No request for money, no matter how small or large or serious or frivolous, could be made before these "presents" were communicated with sincerity and respect to my Aunt Ella. She had gone from our midst years and years ago, even before I was born. But Aunt Ella had remembered me and my mother.

From the first memory of time, sitting at the table covered by a cloth of many colours and by a white linen cloth on Sunday (which she said she had "borrowed" from the Marine!), I would write this monthly dictation of love and respect and request. From that time, and until the time I would leave the country, a letter came to us, with the strange postage stamps of the United States of America, in an envelope of red, white and blue trim, with waves of lines to show where and when it had been posted across the seas in the Canal Zone, and when it arrived in the Post Office in the Public Buildings in Town. And it always contained a money order for five American dollars.

At Easter and at Christmas it was ten dollars. Sometimes she sent twenty.

My mother always dictated phrases like, "As I take this pen in hand to write you these tidings," and "I am, dear Aunt Eloise, your loving nephew."

Aunt Ella once sent us a picture of herself. My mother

said, "Boy, this is the woman who senning you to Cawmere. Kiss the ground she walk on, boy. Respect her."

The picture showed her in a long dress, with a smile on her face, and something in her hand. She looked like my mother. My mother said, "She more older than me, though." But my mother never told me how old *she* was. And I never asked. She was always telling me, "Ask no questions, hear no lies!" Or she would say, "Dogs amongst doctors," which puzzled me. When that was said by an older person, I knew instinctively that it was time to leave the adults to themselves and seek my own level of company.

I never did find out or appreciate the association the old people made between dogs and doctors. It would be years before I would come across signs which read: *Indians and dogs not allowed*; and *Blacks and dogs not allowed!*

SEVEN

Hitler must have been winning the war, for all of a sudden sugar, which we produced, was rationed. It became almost impossible to get and very difficult to buy, unless the shopkeeper liked you. Flour, rice, corn meal for making *cou-cou*, a delicious weekend delicacy, matches, butter from Australia, salt beef and English potatoes — all of a sudden these foodstuffs disappeared from Barbados.

As her morning working hymn, Delcina chose one written for the burial of the dead. *Now the labourer's task is o'er.*

People in the village counted the number of dead at sea. They memorized the famous battles, and the names of the local dead in the air, serving with the Royal Air Force — for some of our men were now flying in the air like birds, Delcina said, all over Germany. But those who fought on land took the heaviest toll.

When Delcina heard all these tragedies in the news, she raised her voice higher and sweeter, singing the burial of the dead.

> *There the tears of earth are dried;*
> *There its hidden things are clear;*
> *There the work of life is tried*
> *By a juster Judge than here.*
> *Father, in Thy gracious keeping*
> *Leave we now Thy servant sleeping.*

"And in case none of wunnuh don't know, I singing hymn number four hundred and one, in *Hymns Ancient and Modern!*" she told the village. Food became as scarce as the news of victories.

Every night on the BBC World News we listened to the voice of Winston Churchill.

We turned to the green bushes among us. "If you don't have a horse," my mother said, "ride a cow." So we made teas from the bushes we normally left growing wild. Miraculous Bush made into tea was suddenly discovered to be good for the bowels. We ground sweet potatoes into flour. With the help of home-made graters, cassava root — both the "poisonous" cassava and the "sweet" cassava; and we turned these formerly despised roots into the most delicious "stable" foods.

At a certain time of night, we had to turn down our kerosene lamps. Black-outs reached us from up in the Mother Country and the various "theatres of war." The Germans, the British said, were now in Caribbean waters. We got scared. *Sireens* sounded throughout the night, throughout the country. Searchlights would point into the sky at nightfall; we would follow the line and imagine German planes in it, and shoot them down with our mouths.

The three or four hundred men who were enlisted in the Barbados Volunteer Force were called into barracks at the Garrison, to prepare themselves for the defence of the British Empire and to eat bully-beef and biscuits.

All of a sudden we had an army. The police were put on alert. Sea scouts became self-important, as they were taken deeper out into the harbour and told a few things about spotting enemy ships by the harbour police. And we heard that our leader, Grantley Adams, sent a cable up to the King, His Britannical Majestical George the Sixth, King of England, Northern Ireland and the British Possessions Beyond the Seas, and told the King, "Go on, England, Little England is behind you." And from that day we were known with pride or embarrassment as "Little England."

41

The ships which contained our new school books and the corn beef and butter from Australia were sunk on the black oily seas between here and there. Students at high schools began to borrow textbooks and copy out the entire books in longhand.

Hitler, the watchman at the Marine, was fired. He was caught by the head watchman with a paperbag of flour. He said he was taking it for his wife and seven children. The women in the village clapped their hands and said, "Serve the bastard right! Hitler used to report us for bringing out a chicken wing from the Marine. The thiefing bitch!"

We continued to write the names of German generals and paint swastikas along the church wall. Some of my friends who were still at St. Matthias School said the list of the dead and those lost at sea grew longer every day. Morning assemblies were spent reading out these lists of the dead and singing *Ride on, ride on, in Majesty*, and in floggings.

And all of a sudden at Combermere a stranger appeared among us. Our new headmaster. He was a drill sergeant of a man. For discipline and "administering" public floggings. We likened him to Himmler. He was military in bearing, tall as the casuarina trees in the grounds at the Marine Hotel; severe and cruel, both in looks and action. He became overnight the Gestapo of the secondary schools in the country.

According to those masters who feared and disliked him, he was recently demobilized from the British Army, Colonial, Dominion & Overseas. The masters called him, in our presence, "that tall, lanky Limey." He looked as devastating in his moustache as Barclay's Bank in Town. He had a most un-Barbadian name. We did not know whether he was a Christian-minded man like our dear former headmaster, the Reverend Armstrong. But he conducted prayers in the hall and made us sing hymns only from the book *Hymns Ancient and Modern*, as the Reverend used to do.

For the five years I was at Combermere I never saw the British Major dressed in anything but the suit of British officers' khaki, without pips. He would thunder down the corridors in brown boots made from alligators or elephants. I did not think he liked any of us. We did not hate him. We didn't see him as a human being. He was an Englishman, sent down to us by the King or our leader or Churchill. He drank more rum in one day than anybody else on the teaching staff, so the masters said.

During these tough war days, my life became more organized. At five minutes to nine we assembled in the hall. We sat on the long wooden benches without backs, and we whispered about the tragedies and achievements of our little world. One day was like the next. Lists of the dead at sea, in the air and on land. We talked like ventriloquists so that the prefects at the head of the rows of benches would not give us "demerits for talking at Prayers."

The assistant masters, who had been ordered to come to Prayers, stood against the south wall and looked bored. The British Major had pinned a command on the Notice Board: all assistant masters were to leave the Common Room, where they played draughts or threw dice or talked about the women and men of the previous night. The first morning after this command, we saw several assistant masters for the first time in years. We thought some of them had been in wheel chairs in all this time of absence from Prayers.

Every morning five hundred of us sang hymns and listened to the short prayer from the *Book of Common Prayers*. We heard about the King and his ministers and that they should be spared from the Germans to lead us better; then we were dismissed.

When the Major wanted to "administer" a public flogging,

the Lower School was "dismissed." The war was still raging overseas. The only evidence we had of it at Combermere was the Major's British khaki uniform without the pips of rank. This strange Englishman, this Major formerly of the British Army, read no notices of the war at assembly; and he did not show us the deeds and the exploits of the Allies. He seemed to know that the war had taken a turn for the worse, for the Allies. School now became a regiment.

At St. Matthias the headmaster was still ringing his dinner bell. Two teachers would pull out the large Map of the World, then the headmaster showed them the current "theatres of war."

"Now, boys, what is the capital of Englan'?"

At the top of their voices the boys are still yelling, "London!"

"And who is the Allies?"

"Englund and Russia and the British Empire, sir!"

The headmaster would still be smiling; and running his chalk-covered hand with the tuning fork in it, his beloved tuning fork, over the wide expanse of the millions of square miles painted in red.

"What my hand passing over now, boys?"

"The British Empire, sir!"

They know, as I knew it, with their eyes shut.

The headmaster is still smiling in that school and looking gratified. He is smiling as if he is the owner of this vast empire of land, known to them by name and by position on a map.

"That is why the sun can never set on the British Empire!"

All those strange countries and cities and people whose languages we did not know but whose positions on the Map of the World we were taught to learn by heart!

Sometimes, in a good mood, when his roses had won First Prize at the annual Agricultural Exhibition, or when he had flogged half the school with his soaked black snake and was washed in perspiration of all the torment he had brought from his home that morning, my old headmaster would gather a few of us, the "good boys," around the globe. He would spin it around on its axis like a top, according to the geography book, and would complete one revolution in a slow spin. And we would see only the red of the British Empire with our unbelieving eyes. So large an empire, to which the headmaster told us we as free people belonged! *Our* empire!

But the British Major did not tell us we belonged to the empire, not in that way.

"Prefects, take posts!"

It was a hot Monday morning. It had rained all weekend. Our school uniforms were damp. The school became silent and stiff. Like a concentration camp. The head boy and the assistant head boy took up their positions on either side of the headmaster's table on the platform. The Major stood like a general in the middle of the platform. Behind him I saw the three large French windows, always open to let in a breeze from the playing field and the canal at the edge of the field. The canal flowed slowly, floating the silt and guts and bodies of dead frogs and chickens, and children killed before birth, so said some boys who lived in that district. It curdled our blood to hear such stories.

The Major was now like Goebbels. People were talking in whispers about the Jews and the concentration camps. It was mentioned one night at the end of the BBC World Service news. The house captains (we called the houses "sets": A, B, C and D) and the prefects stood in front of the plat-

45

form, on our level, facing the trembling culprits, those boys who were to be flogged publicly. The assembly was now quiet, as a court-martial.

Suddenly the shouts and laughter and screams of students from the private school across the street came in on us. We envied their rejoicing and softer discipline. A passenger bus changed gears and when the motor was quieter, we heard shouts and cursing, and a hawker singing out, "Get your okras, yuh yams, yuh eddoes, yuh nice bananas. . . You want me, mistress?"

The Major was furious.

"Armstrong, R. D., mentioned three times, *four* strokes!" he bellowed.

And little Armstrong tried to pull his shirt as far out of his pants as he could in the short frightening time from the bench to the steps of the guillotine. As he climbed the scaffold of three steps, he loosened his belt. If he had more time, he would have wet his face at the tap in crocodile tears and put himself at the mercy of the court, hoping that the sound of the tamarind rod on his mildewed khaki uniform would make such a loud noise and fool the Major-General. But the Major intended to brutalize the small boy.

We sat and anticipated the force and venom of the falling tamarind rod. We counted the number of blows with our eyes closed. Armstrong's eyes were closed even more tightly after the first blow. But we knew that Armstrong was tough, was a "man." He was brave. He was not going to be a little boy and cry. Not in front of three hundred boys. . .

". . . *one afternoon after school, when the headmaster had already marched across the field to his house, one of the small 'bad' boys got a Gillette razor blade and 'broke and entered' the headmaster's office. He got hold of the collection of freshly cut and trimmed tamarind rods. The headmaster kept them on the top of the cupboard which contained the texts of the French course he taught to the fifth form. This 'bad' boy, now a school hero, screwed each rod in the middle just deep enough below the brown skin to make them breakable and weak in the Major's hand. At the next 'administering' of a public flogging we all laughed under our breaths. The older boys said it was after that that the headmaster commanded the porter to get bamboo to flog us with. He had served in the Malaya theatre of war, the head boy told us. . . "*

. . . the tamarind rod breaks in his hand after it flashes back from Armstrong's back. We laugh because some boy has put a tamarind rod in between the bamboo. But just as fast, we are sad again, as the headmaster chooses one long, willowy bamboo from the large collection on his table, beside the *Book of Common Prayer.*

The last boy who faced the Major that morning was mentioned thirty-six times. He got thirty-seven lashes for having been mentioned thirty-six dishonourable times. And when the Major's hand fell on the boy's black backside for the thirty-seventh time, it was no less vicious and stinging than the first blow which Armstrong's khaki pants had reported more than one hour earlier.

That morning I became very sad for the freedom of our country. I wondered if the war would ever end. I waited for the BBC World Service news to tell me when Hitler was going to blow the Allies from the North Atlantic. I wondered when this demobilized Major was going to take a boat and sail back to England.

At the end of the morning, we were all crying real tears: those who were flogged and those who had escaped the Major's wrath. A young, very popular master, pretty with a football at centre forward, as he was pretty with a cover drive on the cricket pitch, broke down and cried. He cried in front of all of us. He had been made to stand and witness his brother receive thirteen of the most vicious blows anybody outside of a prison or a slave plantation or a movie about penal institutions had ever received. The British Major! That tall lanky Limey!

EIGHT

I was now in the third form. Life was becoming even more serious. A civil servant, a sanitary inspector, an overseer, an elementary school teacher, were coming into the focus of my educational accomplishments. I was placed twentieth out of thirty boys. I was under a chloroform of learning things which made no immediate sense. Trigonometry was too hard for my head. We were introduced to the prose of Julius Caesar; and the verse of Vergil. A master who taught us English literature ranted and raved before us in his love for Keats and Byron and Shelley and Milton.

I wondered about my Aunt Ella in the Canal Zone alone without the Empire to protect her. Did my letter get through the German blockade? And I wondered about Milton, a boy in my village who did not know about paradise lost and regained, and who was not blind, and who was an expert at killing lizards and ground doves. "You'll remain the savages you are if you don't read the English poets!" I wondered whether Milton knew there was another Milton.

We learned French.

Je suis, tu suis, il suit. . .

"How many years have you, man?"

"I have thirteen, old man!"

"How are you carrying yourself?"

"I see you remember the reflective verb!"

"I carrying myself well, old man!"

The cow that jumped over the moon; and Mr. Twirly and Mr. Twisty, the two English screws, were now years behind me in elementary school.

We learned "big" things at Combermere. Now we memorized things about a Grecian urn; learned about a man with "resolution and independence" who walked beside a sea and picked up seashells. We picked welts and "sea beefs" ourselves. The fools in our village and the doting old women had been doing this all their lives, and nobody in Barbados wrote a poem about their antics. They were committed to the Jenkins Mental Hospital.

Hannibal, whom we loved (and no one told us he was black like us!) climbed mountains and was smart. Alas, he lost one eye: *in occulo altero*. But he had crossed the Alps, one of the highest mountain ranges in the whole whirl! We loved Hannibal. The name was pure romance and *poultry* in our mouths. We named our pets and our favourites at home Hannibal; and we walked about the school yard spouting *impedimenta* and *transgresserat*, and when we couldn't remember more by heart, we settled on *depuis longtemps*. We continued asking ourselves, "How many years have you?"

And in all this time not a word from the British Major about the Allies and their fights and battles. We didn't know at first that Mussolini was an Italian, a Roman. All the Italians we knew were in books, dead; speaking a dead language; and wearing togas, and eating while lying on their sides: grapes from a bunch and wine from an urn. So why a Grecian urn and not a Roman one?

We in Barbados drank rum. We loved the Italians (and hated Mussolini) because they were like us, like the men in our village who loved rum and women more than work. And the Romans, like our own men, talked and sang hymns ancient and modern all drunklong.

In geography classes we learned the exact place where the rancid butter we ate came from; and the potatoes which we called "English" potatoes; and the rotten, "high" skinny-bodied salt fish: Australia, Idaho and Newfoundland. We had

49

heard that some of our men had emigrated to a place called Africville, in Halifax, to love and to live and to work on gifts of land that was rocks.

Sailors from English ships in the harbour came among us and kicked us and bruised our shins and called us darkies; and didn't say, "Sorry, old boy!" as we had been taught to say on the playing field by the British Major.

We played against them and beat them. They sometimes refused to obey the umpire's decision. It was not the same game we were taught. It was not cricket. But they were the English, the Mother Country's men who were giving up their lives, "on beaches, in the trenches," to keep us safe and free and the entire world civilized and democratic.

One afternoon I stood beside one of these English sailors on the touchline of the football field at Combermere. He had a "hand" of bananas in his hand. Ten fat and juicy things. As the game progressed, I saw him eat all of them except one. Then with a flick of his hairy wrist he threw the banana thirty yards into the canal. It would take days to float among the other obstacles in the foul water, unmolested, down into the harbour to the sea, where his man-of-war lay sleeping in Carlisle Bay. His arms were hairy like the monkeys' in our books and had many blue-painted pictures on them. Some looked like arrows piercing a heart; and some were naked women; and there was one picture that looked like a coat of arms.

"I say, old chap," he said to me, "are there any whores nearby?"

Even then I knew from the schoolboy gossip that the whores in Town did not like the English sailors. "Them Limeys? They too blasted cheap!"

With the help of the whores' experiences, we knew that the English was a strange tribe of economizing men. They were cheap, the whores said. Cheapness came to mean English. But in the classes at Combermere we were taught that the best things were made by the English. English-made. Made in England. The clothes we wore; the books we read; the pencils we wrote with; the Quink ink; the book bags; the combs made from tortoise-shell, which were too fine-toothed for our thick, nappy hair; the medicines, and the Ferrol; the Wincarnis wine which every self-respecting mother gave to her son as a tonic, one spoonful every morning. And the neckties; the perfumes, Evening in Paris and Cush-Cush; the skin powders; and the Brilliantine which made our heads shine, slicked back, concealing the African kink in our hair. *Rule Britannia, Britannia rules the waves. . .*

"For advertisers, the turn-of-the-century fad for all things imperial was a godsend. The Empire was a permanent source of second-hand excitement, a stage-show of exploration and warfare with all suffering either romanticized or removed. In the clothes suggested by the 'Queen, Empire and the British Character,' manufacturers had ideal material: dramatic, colourful and flattering to patriotic self-esteem."

The mustard in the bright-yellow tin of Colman's mustard, with its red lettering, was used in our kitchen. But more often the tin was acquired already empty. My mother would wash it clean with Sunlight soap, from the memory of Queen Victoria, because it was the best soap sold in Barbados. While we used Queen Victoria's mustard, there was another Britannic Majesty on the Throne of England — George the Sixth. The people who made Sunlight were "soap makers by special appointment to Her Majesty," and they forgot to change the boast when the new monarch came along.

Every first Sunday of the month my mother bathed me in a large tub made of wallaba wood, and scrubbed me clean with Pears soap. Once I saw the soap before it was opened and I read in amazement the short history on its label: *Nelson the hero of Trafalgar and Pears soap have become the most familiar names in the English language.*

I knew Nelson. He was the man who had shouted, "England expects every man to do his duty!" He was shot by a cannon ball, and was dying on a ship when he said these brave words. At that time I did not know he was a fornicator. Had Miss Smith, my Sunday School teacher, known this, she would have thrown the Bible at his sinfulness. She would have prayed for him too.

Nelson's expectation of duty was written in the history books and at the base of his statue which stands in the middle of our capital, Bridgetown, looking out to sea, "to see what he can see," as we used to say when we passed the statue.

Nelson had been dead for hundreds of years but every small boy in Barbados giggled in the suds of his memory and history. We would stand in the middle of a fishing boat, or perhaps with luck in life, on the deck of a schooner, and shout, "Little England expects every man to do his duty!"

We were English. The allegiance and patriotism that our leader, Mr. Grantley Adams, had imprisoned us with had been cabled to the Colonial Office in London. We were the English of Little England. Little black Englishmen.

Our masters at Combermere spoke with the accents of the gentlemen of England. When one of the younger masters passed the examination, the Intermediate to the Bachelor of Arts Degree, *External* — an examination which was set and corrected in England — all of a sudden he became very intelligent and educated. Because he was our master and we too wanted to be educated, we spoke like little black Englishmen.

We had in our midst the British Major, a "true-true" Englishman, on whom to pattern the strange inflections of spoken English. We could not know, because of the vast Atlantic which separated us from England, that the speech we were imitating was really working-class London fish-sellers' speech. We, the black aristocracy of an unfree society, exchanged our native speech for English working-class patois!

We stopped going home to eat and instead had suppuh and dinnuh. We began having luncheon. And of course a cuppa toy!

One afternoon I tried out my new language on my mother. She had just told me, "Boy, come and drink this little warm chocolate-tea before it get cold. I put some flour drops in it to help cloid you. Times still hard, boy. The war on. But where there's a will, there's a way, praise God."

"I would prefer a cuppa toy, Ma," I told her.

"Boy, you gone mad?"

I preferred a cuppa toy, for I was a Combermere boy, trained to be a snob, coached to be discriminating. A cuppa toy was better than a cup of rich chocolate. England drank toy, and Little England should too.

And we took pills, Beacham's pills. The language on the box extolled England's greatness. And that was all we needed to recover from whatever deadly illness had forced us to take these pills. The price, "a guinea a box," did not stand in the way of our loyalty. We knew and believed that "nought shall make us rue, if England to itself do rest but true and takes Beacham's pills."

NINE

Suddenly something happened. It was a great event. And one afternoon, just as light turned into dusk, my mother, who had a knack for the dramatic, who feared the darkness more than she feared centipedes, took me into her dark bedroom to explain the seriousness of the event.

"We moving," she said.

The bedroom was secret, silent and voiceless. It was exactly half the size of the small house. In the gloom of the room, I could see the smile on my mother's face. I could feel the relaxation of the tension I had imagined in her body for all these years. I could smell the aroma of Pears soap on her soft, satin, black body.

"We moving," she said again and burst out laughing.

Those two simple words meant that all the years of "sufferation," all the years of working at the Marine, had at last come to an end. And it was the end she had silently worked for. *Rule Britannia!*

"We moving up the hill, Flagstaff Hill."

I thought of Delcina, whose hymns I would no longer hear unless I visited her.

"Yuh father" (she called him that) get a piece o' land to rent. We going work the land, plant canes and a few yams and eddoes, and a head or two o' sweet potatoes. We will be living in this same house, but boy, in good time, in God's *good time. . .* praise God! . . . we intend to turn this *one-roof* into a *two-roof.* After five years or so, we fixing up and adding on a wall front and a big open gallery. Them is my dreams. Them is my dreams, son." Then she broke down and cried.

That evening she allowed me to go out to play long after the fowls had jumped up on their roosts, long after the road was dark. There was no moon that night. Hitler — now a policeman and living in the barracks near the Garrison close to the Army of volunteered board-rifled soldiers who ate bully-beef — came ticking across the road, clothed in his night issue of detective black. He was on a three-speed bicycle.

In my circle of friends with Briggs, Mickey, Johnny and George-Ben, I talked about our new house. They did not envy me: they were too happy for that; they could visit me and eat all the sugar cane they wanted. They saw my new status as their own.

Then we talked about Combermere School. Mickey, Johnny and Briggs were going there now. I imitated the Major's walk and accent. They imitated my imitation. We talked about Hannibal crossing the Alps; we told George-Ben about Livy and Virgil and Caesar, and about a man named Ovid.

"Milton get a job," Mickey said.

"Yeah, Milton is the assistant gardener up at the Marine," Briggs explained.

"Milton, man!" I said, not really sure if I was glad that his long unemployment was now over.

The war was still raging on land, on sea and in the air, so Churchill said every night on the BBC World Service news. We continued to listen to the sombre voice of the BBC announcer, as we stood under George-Ben's aunt's window. We listened to the accent and tried to imitate it, and sometimes we missed the names of the battles and the advances and invasions in the "theatres" of war, and the statistics of the dead.

One night the total number dead in one battle somewhere

in France — we missed the name and the French pronunciation — terrified us. There were more dead in that one battle, more dead men in the war, than living inhabitants and *tourisses* in Barbados.

"If I was Hitler," someone said, "if I was Hitler — I don't mean *we* Hitler the policeman, but the Nazzie, the one up in Germany — I would go 'cross at Sin-Matthias School right now, and with my Luffwoff drop a blasted bomb on that cruel headmaster. He more cruel than the SS. Man, since you left that school, that man has beat the *whole* school at least ten times! Every boy get at least two lashes. Only because the *Hood* and *Nelson* and another ship I can't remember by name went to the bottom. Sink. In the Atlantic. This war is a funny thing."

"He made the whole school stannup one afternoon. Then three minutes o' silence. That lasted almost half day. That day he read the *Advocate* to the whole school. He told us we was fortunate to be British. And at the end of the day we had to sing 'God Save the King' ten times."

"At Cawmere we don't sing 'God Save the King' so often."

"Cawmere is a big school. Yuh don't do little stupid things at a big school. If my father wasn't dead, I sure I would be a Cawmere boy too."

"All we got to do at Cawmere is learn a few lines o' Latin from Vergil, recite a poem like *Fair Daffodil we hate to see thee haste away so soon. . .*"

"What is a daffodil, though? They have daffodils at Cawmere?"

"A daffodil? A daffodil is only the name of a flower, man!"

"But we got flowers growing all over the place, wild flowers and good flowers. In the school garden and *out the front road*. And why we never call them a daffodil?"

"A daffodil is a English flower!"

"We is English too, man."

"One of these days I am going up in the Mother Country to further my studies."

56

"Who you prefer? Churchill or Hitler?"

"I prefer Churchill more better than Hitler. Although Hitler have prettier newniforms."

"Me too."

"The SS uniforms more prettier than the British Army uniforms."

"The headmaster say we belong to the Allies, that the Axes is murderers."

"The reason why I like Churchill so bad is that I hear Churchill is a man who could talk in the House o' Commas all day and night, and then hold-on 'pon a bottle o' liquor and before you say *Mississippi*, that bottle drink-off! Down the hatch. I hear too from Profit, the fellow working on boats that travel all over the Atlantic and the Suez Canal, that Churchill is a man who didn't even finish school. He didn't pass in Latin. That's why I think that Churchill is a bigger giant than Hitler."

"What about Goering?"

"Tha's the fellow in charge of the Luffwuff? He?"

"None o' them can't touch the SS, though! With the SS, all you got to do is *dream* about committing a crime, like spying or sabotage, and before you wake up, the SS got you tied down and pulling out your damn fingernails!"

"That is what I call real torture, boy! The Nazzies invent torture."

"Hitler the policeman torture Milton last Friday for stealing a cake o' soap from the drug store out the front road. Hitler gave Milton two bull-pistle lashes. Talk 'bout local torture? Go and see our Hitler!"

"Between Churchill and Hitler then. The Allies and the Axes."

The voting was to begin.

"Those in favour of Hitler and the Nazzies?"

Two of us put up our hands.

"Who for Churchill and the Allies?"

The other two raised their hands.

I was the chairman. In my wild small world of international

affairs, and of the British House of Commons debates, I did not know that the chairman had a casting vote. So the vote was tied through my ignorance; and the power which I could have used in my office under the street lamp wilted.

"It's much of a muchness then," George-Ben said. He shrugged both shoulders.

And we went home to bed, and to drink cocoa-tea with flour drops in it, and to say in our dark homes, *Our father who art in heaven.* And to rub our feet together before we got into bed, to wipe off the dust of the road. And to hope that we did not wet our beds that night. Before I went to sleep, I wondered what the Nazzies drank just before they went to bed.

Hammers pounded like ack-ack guns against the side of the house. Large wood ants and other eaters of wood spurted out of the grey holes like surrendering enemy troops. They were coming at me, crawling all over my bed and into my eyes. They started to eat me alive. I was Gulliver in a pool of honey and blood and Lilliputians. The pounding grew louder. It turned into cannon fire. And then it stopped.

I opened my eyes. The carpenter of the village and some helpers had come to move the house. I found myself in the four-poster bed, half-sunken like a submarine, amongst the soft cush-cush grass of the mattress. I had inherited my mother's bed that night. My mother and stepfather had stayed up packing plates and spoons, knives and forks, cups and saucers, most of which we used only at Easter and Christmas; and putting them in old newspapers. The tots and enamel plates, our daily cutlery and common China, were thrown into boxes.

Beside the house, just under my window, was a jackass

braying and stomping at flies and eating the top of my mother's Miraculous Bush tree. The flies on the jackass's face were sucking his eyes and mouth.

Flies were everywhere, like the morning wind. Centipedes in the wet ground squirmed as if the ground itself was moving. In the middle of the yard, after the paling had been taken down, galvanized sheets were packed one on the other. They looked like a large metallic concertina. On this concertina of galvanized sheet was a bucket of fresh water covered by a cloth. The fowls, the two fowl-cocks and the chickens were still in their coops.

The pig was grunting and shining like vaseline from his bath. He had been washed by my mother. She had bought a "part" in this pig. Village custom said that since she paid no money for the pig, she could feed it in her yard; and when it was killed, which it was going to be on a Saturday before Easter, half would be hers.

Such arrangements caused fights among my mother and the neighbours. For in the verbal arrangements, sometimes no one remembered to specify which half of the pig he wanted. Each partner wanted the half with the head. Custom said that to cut a pig in half along the spine was unthinkable and foolish. Each partner demanded the "biggest" half. This half was more suitable for making the local dish of "black pudding and souce." The half with the head gave you the liver and *harslick* and brains and eyes, to be fried deep in lard oil, made brown and hard when it was floured; and the liver and *harslick* would be greasy and delicious as a sucked finger on a Saturday afternoon. It was served with a bowl of mellow, rich, yellow turned meal, cou-cou. Any woman who would not declare war to claim the biggest half, the half with the head, would be a woman "with rocks in her own head."

Our Christian respect for Sunday said that demolishing and moving the house could not begin until after Matins. Women and men would be home from church. A heavy hot meal of peas and rice and baked pork would be served to the workmen and the family, all of us eating in a democratic picnic in the yard on the ground. There would be large quantities of rum and rum punch.

The "carpenter" and men who helped with the moving belch many times and tell a few dirty jokes about moving houses.

It is now long past the middle of the afternoon, and the flies are less universal. The jackass is sleeping at a quiet standstill. The house is collapsed, taken apart board by board, each nail saved for its reconstruction. The men are panting and hungry again. My mother serves lemonade and corn beef and biscuits. The lemonade looks brown and the piths of limes float among the ice.

The jackass is harnessed in its cart. Each board is loaded and labelled, so that with the drink and the sun and the long journey, the carpenter would not nail a window in the place made for the front door — or fasten the front door to the back of the house.

Our carpenter was not a trained craftsman. He was a man who walked around the village with a saw and hammer in his hand. He learned his trade as he made mistakes on the houses of his friends and neighbours, and made them all into his enemies. My mother watched him as if he were a spy. She hated carpenters more than he hated centipedes.

The last floor board was ripped up. All of a sudden my mother screamed. We thought it was her sadness for having to move from St. Matthias. Everybody stood dead. Then a man cried out, "Good Jesus Christ!" As he jumped back, a nail ripped his khaki trousers and blood spurted.

My mother was like a mahogany figurine, staring at the ground. She could have been dead, stricken by a "heart affection," for she had warned us about her heart many times before. When movement returned to her body, she pointed.

In the middle of the ground, where her bedroom was, in the thick rich brown earth, were a million fat, squirming centipedes.

"By Sin-Peter and by Sin-Paul," my mother gasped.

60

"Good Jesus Christ!" the carpenter said.

Looking at them I could feel their deadly sting. Once I got a sting near my eyes. The pain was so great I wanted to gouge out my eyes. Once in our village a centipede crawled into a baby's mouth and came out through the nostril.

"By Sin-Peter and by Sin-Paul!" My mother was shouting now. She always thought this invocation could render the centipedes immovable and give her time to get the clothes iron, a hammer or a shoe. But these were millions. "Something, quick-quick-quick! Boy, oh-Christ, you so-damn-slow! Something-to-kill-these-blasted-barmints-with. . . "

The carpenter poured kerosene on them. And when he threw the match, my mother shook her head in disbelief and watched the crackling awful-smelling barbecue. . . .

We started out, now almost dusk, along St. Matthias Road, rutted and gutted, and rounded the corner where Mickey and George-Ben and Johnny and Briggs lived, where we used to stand and talk ourselves into arguments and philosophies about the war.

The donkey took the hill where Miss Haynes, the best maker of coconut bread in the village, lived; and we passed that bend in the road, climbing slowly. I took a last whiff of the bread that used to rise like a lifeboat in the cool dark nights.

My mother walked beside me, saying something about "blasted santapees so big and so many. I hope they ain't got none in Flagstaff Road!"; and mumbling about the sloth of the jackass as we walked behind it.

My stepfather walked in front, proud, beside the jackass's uncontrollable braying, *honk-hee-eee-honk*!; and the carpenter walked on the other side of the jackass's ears.

To the men and women hanging around the Bath Corner, the four of us must have appeared like travellers from a faded colour illustration in the *Bible Stories for Children*. Miss Smith could put us into that biblical past of travellers.

The carpenter was talking about cricket and holding the "snuff bottle," the improvised light made from a bottle with kerosene in it and a cloth wick stuffed into the neck of the bottle. Not even a hurricane could blow it out.

The sun that bids us rest is waking
Our brethren 'neath the western sky,
And hour by hour fresh lips are making
Thy wondrous doings heard on high.

"That is Delcina, ain't it?"

"Lord, look how that woman voice reaching us all up here!"

"The day thou gavest Lord is ended," my stepfather said. He sang tenor in the church choir. "She just sing the fourth verse." And he picked up the hymn with her, from that distance, as she moved into the fifth and final verse, raising his voice in a delightful tenor part — with the carpenter handling the bass line and my mother humming along because she did not know the words. . .

Thy Kingdom stands and grows forever,
Till all Thy creatures own Thy sway.

I knew the last verse too.

"Delcina pick a proper hymn to see us off with," my mother said. "God bless her."

We reached the noisy stretch of the road. On one side were the joiner-shops where they made furniture out of mahogany, the pride of the village. These joiners got First Prize every year at the annual Agricultural Exhibition.

We passed a house of "no repuke," my mother called it, then the rum shop where the "demons, those Nicodemons of worthless mens and womens" drank snaps of rum and gambled all day and night, and where sometimes we would catch a glimpse of Hitler the policeman throwing a snap of rum straight down his parched throat, while trying to hide in his uniform.

Then the Bath Corner itself. Tonight, Profit, my hero from birth, is talking about high seas and high waves: ". . . yuh see the top o' that building there! Not the Christian Mission Church, yuh cunt! . . . " My mother glanced in my direction. "Goodnight, mistress! I see yuh moving . . . the *next* one, the building next to it. That! Well, I have been on a ship coming through the Darnells, and be-Jesus Christ, when I tell you a *wave*, well I mean. . . "

And we pass on our journey, and just before we leave him, Profit's voice is beside us, interrupting his tale. "Night, Lukey! Lukey, boy, you moving away from we, eh, boy? God go with you. . . "

We pass a church, not an Anglican church but one of a different colour, as my mother calls it; of a different denomination. The singing is loud and beautiful, reaching a high getting-into-the-spirit pitch. Women are screaming *Glory and Hallelulia*, jumping off the benches into the air and onto other benches, and I can hear the floorboards shaking.

My mother took me to this very church one night during revival time. It was a humid, rainy Friday night, and I saw for the first time the sisters' panties and their luscious legs. I saw the deacons froth at the mouth; and I saw how Brother Taylor watched them, the men and the women, like a man possessed. Brother Taylor had froth at his mouth too. That night he spoke a poetry of brimstone and ashes and warned the gambling *mens and womens in this evil-evil whirl; you is the demons and Nicodemons of the coming of the Lord. Brothers and sisters, the coming is at hand! Prepare yuh-selves! I say, God ain't asleep. When He come, don't let He find wunnuh in a doze from drinking snaps of that demon, rum. . .*

Tonight he was shouting as we passed abreast of his sermon, which sometimes lasted for four hours in the wet, shirt-smelling trembling church.

A man is in the gutter. He is too drunk to bear the weight of his legs, and has fallen just within the distance of hearing Pastor Taylor's fire and the rock-stones in his voice.

Suddenly a passenger bus bringing people home from the last show at the Olympic Theatre appears around the corner, and the lights from the bus wake up the jackass who starts to move faster and to bray. . . The drugged jackass moves farther into the road than he should. Brakes screech. The bus conductor jumps off from the running-board like a ballerina, a butterfly, like a man at a dance at the Marine. He lands erect on the tar road. The large leather pouch in which he keeps the bus fares is held close to his chest.

"Why the five o' wunnuh don't move outta the rass-hole road!"

And as if he hadn't spoken, he jumps back onto the creeping running-board as the bus pulls away up the road.

My mother's hand finds mine in the dark road. "Demons and Nicodemons!" she says. "Shut your ears 'gainst the blasphemies in this land."

Two boys hop onto the bus, catching a free ride for ten yards only. The conductor sees them and screams, "Get to-shite off! Get off!" His voice fades. And Dayrells Road becomes a shadow in the snuff-bottled light and part of a former life.

We turn into Deighton Road and my mother sees me missing steps and walking out of rhythm with the jackass. She lifts me up and I smell her perspiration. She puts me on the cart, on the seat of our outdoor toilet, to rest and sleep.

I see the tops of trees. Bigger shadows. Bigger ghosts. There are no red and gold flowers now, no silken ones, no white ones. The night has no colour. There is only one colour, the shadow of the shaking trees. And the smell of the Lady-of-the-Night flowers. . .

TEN

Flagstaff Road got its name from the flag and staff on which the Union Jack was raised every morning at eight, and pulled down and folded every evening at six, on the look-out to the harbour, by a man whose waist was thicker than his chest. He was a bow-legged man who was in charge of the look-out and talked about nothing but cricket.

When we became friends, he showed me pictures of Don Bradman, the Australian cricketer, making a square cut and a cover drive. When this man was not playing draughts with one of the many unemployed men, he was talking about cricket. He played and talked in the circular wooden look-out, painted green because it was run by the government.

Cover drives and square cuts. Charlie Griffith's fast bowling: an inswinger that travelled at "ninety kiss-me-arse miles an hour, boy!" All this and more he told me about as he stood at the look-out window, higher than any of the other houses that surrounded us, higher than the waves Profit talked about.

He told me he looked through his spyglass for warships and spies and Germans, although the war had ended. "I was the *first* man in this whole island to spot the German submarine that torpedo the *Cornwallis*! Always on the job. I barely catched a glimpse of this thing peeping up above the water, and I say to myself, My God, a submarine, a *parascope*! And *bram*! I call in my report. . . "

He let me look through the spyglass one day, and I saw a woman below the hill, and then a man on the deck of a tourist liner drinking a glass of water. All things became clear and near and beautiful. I could look down into the harbour where other ships had stopped, over the heads of the tennis players at the Garrison Savannah, down the hill in St. Matthias, and into a woman's back yard . . . she bends down, she puts her hands on her hips and lifts her dress, and I hear the sprinkling water on the stones in her yard where she puts clothes to be bleached as she pees. . .

"Jesus Christ, Tom, Don Bradman was a man who could cut a ball offa the centre stump, straight to point, he was so blasted fast with the willow! And you would hear the ball hit the blasted boundary, *blam*! And not a man would move, not a blasted man!"

He smoked a package of Trumpeter cigarettes a day, by lighting only the first one. He took one from his pocket and held it to the stub in his mouth. He threw the stub over the hill.

"Well, lemme tell you 'bout the time Don Bradman was batting, well, look at this picture! You see the grace and the footworks? When I was a man in my prime, playing in League cricket 'bout here, and you see me put on them pads and tek that walk to the wicket. . . Watch me now, how I uses to take guard. Watch. Nothing but centre! I nods my cap to the 'Pire, and from that moment on it is *bram! bram! plax! bram!* . . . Them is fours! All fours. And offa the fastest bowling in island! Axe anybody 'bout me."

It was time to take another cigarette from his pocket. "But if my father had the means, if I had come along in your time, with all the privileges you got. . . Boy, I really can't understand why you don't stop all this blasted running round a pasture, as if you is a blasted race horse! Play some cricket, boy. It is a gentleman's game! And you being a Cawmere boy, cricket could take you to the ends of the earth. Take you up the ladder of society. Take you places. I have let

66

you look through that spying glass there, and you see things coming in the harbour. Well, cricket could take you to the places that you can't even see through that blasted cheap spying glass, then! Cricket is a gentleman's game. And you could be a gentleman, travelling all over this blasted Chinee-whirl. . . "

Friends and family had been left behind down the hill in St. Matthias. Some of them had not prospered. Some went to Amurca. But we visited the others often. I was now a choir boy in the Anglican Church. Choir practice was held on Friday nights at seven o'clock. I ran down hills, through three villages, picking and stealing *dunks* on my way, humming descants of Psalms, and memorizing Roman numerals to help me find the Psalms in the *Psalter* we used on Sundays. X's and L's were always the easiest to memorize. And seeing the sea always in front of me, and remembering what I saw when I looked through the spyglass in the look-out.

In the best light of day, just before the sun turns into a red ball and is lost forever, I would walk through pastures of brown dying grass, where sheep with black bellies snapped at the disappearing grass, and stir the occasional sheep or goat, or step on their droppings, like large black soft marbles; frighten fowls out of my way, and walk soft and scared whenever a dog appeared.

And when a dog growled, as all poor dogs in our neighbourhood did, I would run before he could gather his pack of garbage-eating "salmon-tot" pedigreed mongrels and monster after me. Running from these dogs turned me into a champion sprinter at Combermere.

There were always dogs. Thin dogs. Mangy dogs. Fat dogs.

Dogs in heat, stuck together for a day. Mean dogs. Dogs of all colours. There was one dog in each village which was known as the meanest.

Dogs were kept as guards. You kicked a dog to let him know you loved him, to let him know who was master and doctor. And you fed him whatever was left over from the meagre wartime table. You never petted a dog. Somebody might call you a sissy.

Almost all the dogs in Barbados were named Rover. Rover was a dog on Flagstaff Road; and he was a dog in St. Matthias; and he was a dog in Town. *Dogs amongst doctors!*

My mother knew the deep, dark, deadly secrets of dogs. I was terrified of them. They tore my school uniform, always in the middle of the left-hand "seat," always in the shape of an L. The dogs of Belleville Avenue and in the back of Government House were the biggest, meanest dogs in Barbados. They belonged to the rich.

Dogs caused my heart to stop beating. And at night, in their one-eyed sleep, they awoke and chased me for yards of toe-stumping terror.

I never had a dog, nor patted one. *Dogs amongst doctors!* But one afternoon I saw a boy patting a dog along the Hastings Rocks. Tourists and the white people lived there. The boy was white. The dog was black. He patted the dog, and the dog wagged its tail. And then he put his mouth to the dog's mouth and *kissed* him. I turned to the gutter and threw up my dinner.

Before I had reached the Hastings Rocks, I saw a dog eating a dead frog. Our dogs ate dead chickens, sucked rotten eggs and were stoned to death. Sometimes we killed a dog for eating a chicken.

Nobody who lived in our new village, nobody who knew dogs, ever kissed one. But on this bright afternoon, *out the front road*, I noticed for the first time that there were, as my mother would say, "two different and complete tribes o' people living in this place." One tribe kicked dogs, the other kissed them. *Dogs amongst doctors!*

ELEVEN

There were few white boys at Combermere School in these days. The white boys went to Harrison College, "the big school" across the fence from us at Combermere. Or to the Lodge School, which was far in the country district and catered to the rich white sons of plantation owners, managers and absentee landlords, and the sons of English Colonial officers and others who ran the country and the government; also the sons of wealthy Latin American families who wanted their heirs to speak three languages: Latin, American and Barbadian.

The Lodge School was a boarding school. That added to its mystery and charm, and at the same time took it completely out of my reach. We had heard of two black boys who went there, and we were told that they were "very rich and very bright."

Any black boy who achieved brilliance at book learning, who got a job that no one remembered ever being held by a black boy, such a boy was said to be "bright-bright-bright." He was either a "Latin fool," or a "Mathematics fool," or a "Science fool." He was also said to be slightly mad. "Off his head."

All around me there were boys like this, who were "spraining" their brains by always reading. Boys who were going mad because of the things learned in books but who could not discuss with anybody — not with sister, brother, and certainly not with mother and father — any of that book learning.

These bright-bright-bright boys, these "idiots," these *fools*, walked in silence carrying all that book knowledge in their heads, and were regarded with fear and respect. They were the silent acknowledgement that something strange and dangerous was happening among the poor. They walked with their heads bent to the ground.

One of my heroes was such a boy. He had also attended St. Matthias Boys' School. He lived at the top of a hill, near the Bath Corner where Profit and other men who had travelled all over the world — the Middle East, the Far East and the Near East (and as one of them said, "the East-East") — would congregate every night except when the rains came. They took us on tours around the Map of the World, and laid the foundation for our desperate determination to leave the small island-country, the rock on which much of the rumour and ritual of our existence was founded.

This bright-bright-bright boy was a "Mathematics fool." He won a scholarship to Harrison College. Whenever you saw him, if you ever saw him, for many of us talked about him without ever having seen him in the flesh, he was "doing his lessons" and was too busy to talk about kites or cricket or girls. The men who had seen countries and cities bigger than our imaginations never saw him long enough to tell him about these things.

My hero at the top of the hill went to Harrison College carrying big books in his blue English-made school bag. Nobody in the village would consider him to be a real Mathematics fool if the books he chose to bring home from Harrison College were not the biggest books to be seen in the village. Books about theorems and calculus and Pythagoras, books approaching in size the grandeur of the Bible on the church lectern. That Bible was the biggest book most of us had ever seen.

He was a fat boy who would have been given the soft-boiled egg even if there was only one in the house; and the porridge, and the toast made over the small sooty stove; and his lunch would have consisted of bread with the edges trimmed, the trimmings to be saved for his sister, who was not bright-bright-bright and was not expected to be, and not given the chance.

Boys got the best food and attention, and the least floggings, if they were high school boys. Girls were expected to be dressmakers, sugar and silent, spice and stupid, and wash the boys' clothes. So my hero's sister would have helped her mother with the needlework which sustained the family.

In elementary school this bright-bright-bright boy would have done homework. At Harrison College it had become *lessons*. Boys who had promise, boys who had money, took private lessons. And the "private-lessons boys" became a special class, a special caste. They learned about English history, algebra, geography and French. They walked differently. They talked differently. Like little fat black Englishmen. They were given soft-boiled eggs and trimmed sandwiches. Private-lessons boys remained in after school and were taught this extra knowledge in secrecy. I joined the private-lessons tribe.

We belonged to a masonic temple whose rites and rituals were never discussed in the hearing of the ordinary boys. We would sit in two groups. One was preparing for the examination towards a scholarship to Harrison College; the other group, for the examination to get them into one of the two secondary schools, Combermere or the Boys' Foundation School. The examinations were called the Junior to Second Grade, the Senior to Second Grade, the Junior to First Grade, the Senior to Second Grade. These names were given to the examinations by the Colonial Office in London.

From the *History of England*, written by a man named Ransome, we learned about the Battle of Hastings; the Battle of Bannockburn; about Kings who lost their heads; about Kings who kept their heads; and about Kings whose wives lost theirs; about Cranmer; about Parliament; about a Cardinal who, I think, became a Chancellor and who was about to lose his head too and said before the axe fell, "If I had served God half as well as I have served the King, He would not now cause me to lose my head."

We learned about a man who could have been a Barbadian, who wanted to blow up everything, including the King and the Houses of Parliament, and who lost his head. On Guy Fawkes Day we now celebrate him in Barbados by eating *conkies* and blowing up gunpowder and spinning wheels and "bombs." I knew *all* about the Kings; the Tudors, Stuarts and Plantagenets; and the Wars of the Roses; but nothing was taught about Barbados. We lived in Barbados, but we studied English society and manners.

I would walk from those private-lessons classes, past the church which resembled castles in the *History of England* book, and sit at the table with my mother, under the weak kerosene lamp, and hope to live in a castle some day; to speak in Parliament perhaps, wear the same kind of robes as the Cardinal who lost his head. Or to be an archbishop.

Through my training, and my selection into the club of the private-lessons boys, I had already evacuated the small run-down house in which I studied this tragic loss of heads in high places. I was more at ease in England, the Mother Country, than in Barbados. I lived the lives of those great men in the *History of England* book. My mind crawled with battles and speeches, with Divine Rights, Magna Cartas, and I saw myself sitting in ermine with the Lords and Dukes, eating and drinking with Charles the First, who himself got into trouble and paid for it with his head. Being a private-lessons boy was very heady stuff!

The women in the book — Anne Boleyn, Anne of Cleves, Elizabeth Tudor (one by this name lived in Town), Mary Queen of Scots — all these were women with whom I was in love. I painted their faces black and put their huge crino-lined dresses on the girls I saw around me.

I was not a "History fool": I just loved and cherished my past in the *History of England* book. I did not use it as a stepping stone to the Civil Service or the Department of Sanitary Inspection. I decided instead to live it, to make it a part of me.

TWELVE

The Bath Corner. Here I first heard about Hitler and his intentions. Here the comparison between Churchill and Hitler was made. And we, small in the order of knowledge, would memorize each word, each nuance, and agree with the man who had the most colourful way of putting his argument across; who talked the loudest and used the prettiest profane language to sweeten his harsh contentions.

"Hitler is a fucking giant. Hitler isn't no mock-man. Hitler don't mek sport with his enemies. I going tell you something 'bout Hitler now. . . " His voice would trail off while he fished in his pockets for a package of Trumpeter cigarettes.

I felt he was doing this for effect; that if he began his argument with *I going tell you something 'bout Hitler,* and didn't have some stage craft and mannerisms to hold our attention, everybody would walk off.

"I was reading this book one day in the public library," he went on. We knew he had to begin this way, for books and newspapers contained all the knowledge in the whirl. And if any man could read, had the time to walk to Town and sit down and read a book, all those miles from this cor-ner to the public library, he was a serious man, a special man, a dangerous man, a man who, like Hitler, was a blasted giant. This kind of a man was getting too much knowledge without having to pay for it by attending a government secondary school.

He would try to remember the name of the book, and couldn't. It had to be a big book. Big facts were not printed in little books. And certain facts that needed high irrefutable authority could not be quoted from the *Advocate*, an ordinary local newspaper. So the man had to talk about a book he had read in the public library.

"You know why Hitler is a fucking giant?" He paused and allowed us to soak in those words.

We closed our eyes and opened them again, and rolled them around in our heads to look "serious."

In the time we had rolled our eyes around and coughed and looked "serious," he had searched for another cigarette, took it out of the package and knocked its end to stiffen the smoke; lit it, holding the match in his cupped hands, and then he blew the smoke straight out like an accusation into our faces, like a boast of his superior knowledge.

"I am going to tell you why Hitler is a fucking giant. Hitler is a giant because Hitler understand that by beating Englund, Englund would have to let go, free all her colonies and possessions beyond the seas. The people living now in them colonies and territories would become free. People like me-so. And you-so. And the Mathematics-fool-so. I read that in a book in the public library. And I dare any one o' wunnuh to argue against that point. Philosophically speaking, though, Hitler is a giant compare to Churchill."

So when the man at the Bath Corner mentioned the book he had read in the public library, his opponent who had become emotional and had been praising the British Empire, but who had forgotten to say that the self-evident truths he was telling us had *come from a book*, that man lost the argument.

The sea was quiet that night.

The man had seen it in a book. He may never be a student

75

at Harrison College; could not now be one, for he was past nineteen, perhaps twenty-one, for he had a woman "in the family way"; but he had done the next best thing. He studied books.

For days after, we went about the school yard and in our smaller groups, repeating this wise man's contention. And we always made a point in our smaller-scaled arguments, always to begin with the phrase, Philosophically speaking. . .

None of us looked up the word in a dictionary. The word had been printed in the book the man had read. It had won an argument. And it would win many more arguments, merely by being used. *Philosophically speaking, man!*

The men knew I had some knowledge contained in big books. And sometimes I would be called upon to bear the brutal responsibility for the existence of a book mentioned by one of the contenders around the Bath Corner.

"Look," he would say, "if you don't believe *me*, ask Tom. He is a Cawmere boy."

I could understand the lines in a poem, understand what they meant, in metaphor and in literal meaning, and still did not understand the poem. I was living inside the words of poems, in the same way that I lived inside the deeds of Kings and archbishops, without ever knowing the dates of those deeds.

The one recurring date which I had difficulty forgetting was 1066. The Battle of Hastings was fought in 1066. And 1066 became for me the same thing as saying, "Good morning." 1066 meant the beginning of things. Of civilization. Of the world.

There was a certain magic in it for me, in the sound of that date, as if it was the beginning of recorded time. "Man, it happen' *after* 1066!" And in a way, it did. 1066 was, for me, the gate in somebody's paling; and I felt that although that gate was the only entrance, once I had entered it I would see other things inside the paling. I could not be a "History fool" because no other year was so magically important.

And then, too, only a few yards from our house in St. Matthias was the district named Hastings. The Hastings Rocks. There was one Hastings in Barbados; and the other in England. I was close to the possibility of a field of battle. Hastings in Barbados was easily transformed to that other medieval place, and I filled it with soldiers and horses and men and arrows and bows, and I made Mickey and Briggs and Johnny and George-Ben into lords on horses leading foot soldiers into battle; and we fought this battle of our Hastings down to the sea, below the drug store, down the sudden drop, among the beach trees and the coconut trees, among the crab-holes and the sand which moved when you walked on it, like very small ball bearings. . . .

There were twenty-four places in the examination which the "private-lessons boys" took and which could get you a free education at Combermere. The examination was taken at one of the big schools. Parents came dressed as if they were going to church. We private-lessons boys came in ties and cork hats. We were equipped with new bottles of Quink ink, pencil boxes, rulers that had centimeters and millimeters on them, and which always reminded me of centipedes; and some of us even had Esterbrook pens.

At the end of the examination which consisted of English

history and arithmetic, we would be tired and depressed, and scared to know our results. Our shirt pockets would be stained by the fountain pens which always leaked. Our fingers turned blue. But to have ink stains on our fingers was a sign that we were educated. Gardener-boys, like Milton, or boys who fielded tennis balls at the Garrison Savannah Tennis Club, did not have their shirts and fingers stained with Quink ink.

Some parents, especially those who were elementary teachers, would take their children aside and go over the anticipated answers with them. And then these boys would break out crying; and there would be floggings. And some parents would renounce any relationship to their sons. The girls suffered similarly in another part of the island once a year.

More than two hundred boys took the examination when I did. I came twenty-eighth. I was the twenty-eighth most intelligent boy in the country that year in that examination. I was destined to get a share in the country's wealth and promise.

"How you come in the Junior to Second Grade?" the man who told us about Hitler asked me the day the results were published in the *Advocate*.

"Twenty-eight."

"Boy, you bright as shite!"

I became too good overnight to continue at St. Matthias School. To be a waiter at the Marine would now be an insult to one with so much potential. To be a gardener was out of the question. Perhaps, with more private lessons, I too could be a Mathematics fool, and talk pure mathematics, like my hero at the top of the hill.

"Send the boy to Cawmere. Let him study Latin and French," a neighbour told my mother.

"What you want to be?" my mother asked me. Before I answered, she said, "Mechanics work is the best outta all the 'prenticeships going. The joiner-shop by the Bath Corner is another one. But I can't see you sawing wood, especially that

78

hard mahogany wood, all day long in the hot sun. I think that is too hard. Gardener out. I would kill myself first if I was to know even if I was dead . . . Lord beg your pardon . . . that you become one of those boys down there at the Savannah, dressed in a blue suit, and fielding tennis balls that them lawless white people hitting 'bout. I don't know why somebody don't *abolish* things like that."

She was a new woman. Her son had come twenty-eighth. Her son had "blessed her head." Her status was now rising. Women who had passed in front of our small house once a week going to Mothers' Union service at the church, and who even the day before the results were announced passed and didn't speak, these women now stopped and talked and invited her to join them.

I had seen these women, all mothers, always dressed in white, with a Bible tucked under their arms, and sucking cough drops, their heads looking straight ahead as soon as they got to our house.

Now they were stopping and gossiping with my mother about their superiors. We never gossiped about our inferiors. And to be superior or inferior was something only these women could calculate through the amazing arithmetic of status. These Mothers' Union women now stopped and said, "What a nice boy you have, Mother! God have really heard our prayers for you and the boy." My mother hardly knew them. "Didn't you tell me, Mother, that you have a sister in the States?"

And that was when the idea was born. That was the first day I started to write the dictated letters to my Aunt Ella: *As I take up my pen in hand to write these few greetings, I hope that the reaches of them will find you in a perfect state of good health. . .*

THIRTEEN

Flagstaff Road was a dream. And innocent. Men did not congregate around corners or under street lamps at night. They were too tired from working in the fields during the day. There was no tribal, extra-curricular education as by the Bath Corner in St. Matthias. Combermere School was all I had.

With my promotion to a higher form, I started to think of the brand of "fool" I wanted to become — an English fool, a French fool or a Geography fool. But there were already enough bright-bright-bright boys, foolish boys, in my class. It remained for me to be a running fool. I would have to run for my glory, like no one had ever run.

Flagstaff Road and Clapham were wide, unpopulated wilds. The fields of canes, and at some time of year, the fields of corn, covered the golden tops of my barefoot days. There were six houses on our side of the road. At the corner there was a family of old people. No children. They owned a cow, and the woman of the house did not go out to work, or take in ironing for the rich people, or do needlework for money. They had means.

Close by, a couple living together: although no one knew whether they were married. But this village held nothing against the "wife." She stifled all gossip since she was the most famous preacher in the Church of the Nazarene down the main road. Her voice was like honey. When she testified at revival meetings, and you were within the distance of hearing her voice, you were pulled into the church, and her religious conviction made you walk the long journey of personal cleansing to the altar, and you took Jesus as your personal Saviour. You bowed your head in her presence. She was like majesty.

She lived with a man who worked like a miner of rock-stone, in a quarry. He laboured under the smashing sun, under the hill near the look-out, with a six-foot iron drill in his warted, calloused hands. He smelled like limestone and sweat. When he said good morning, you nodded and hoped that he wouldn't shake your hands and break them in his iron grip. If he shook your hands, you had no bones left.

He had recently returned from somewhere. The people didn't say where: perhaps Amurca, perhaps the Panama Canal, perhaps in the States picking oranges during the war, perhaps Glendairy Prison. We said he had just returned from Amurca. His standing in the village was as solid as the drill he drove into the hard ground. We all called him Mr. Thomas.

His "wife" was Sister Thomas to everyone. The title "sister" made her like the blood of the Lamb. Untouchable. She bore no turpitude of social sins. She was the colour of coffee with just too much cream in it. She was young and sexy-looking. Big eyes and big mouth and big legs, which you seldom saw but could imagine.

If you were a young woman in Flagstaff Road, and not married, and were "living with a man" and had children, you took God as your personal Saviour rather than face your neighbours' disapproval. The simple but iron-clad customs of this village told you what to do. You became a "sister" in a church. But not a Church of England. England did not tolerate this native ingenuity. England did not understand.

On our right-hand side, which was the way my mother gave directions, was a large house surrounded by trees. You were somebody if you had trees around your house. If those trees were fruit trees, you had greater power. You could bribe children and adults to run errands for you in a barter for fruits.

The war was on.

You ran errands to the shop for Miss Haynes, or you fetched her a bucket of fresh water from the standpipe. Miss Haynes belonged to no church, and so far as we could guess, to no God. In return for your help, you got a sugar apple or two ripe mangoes or a breadfruit. A breadfruit meant that you had dinner for that day.

Miss Haynes was another Untouchable. She had lived in Amurca. Months would pass and we wouldn't see her. And then all of a sudden there would be hired cars and electric lights burning all night, and in the morning we would see cousins who hadn't existed before. And outside at the back of her paling where she grew acres of corn would be three or four barrels, out of which the treasure from Amurca had been taken.

Miss Haynes was mysterious, unknown to us; but she was friendly. She had gold teeth, top and bottom, in her laughing mouth; and gold bangles on both wrists. Once she gave me a stick of Wrigleys chewing gum. I chewed that stick and enjoyed the strange sensation of refreshed breath for that entire weekend.

She was a black woman. Sister Thomas was brown-skinned and had freckles. These two women never exchanged one word between them. They had probably met when they were in Amurca, in some bad experience, my mother said. Or they might have been cousins. I grew up knowing cousins who didn't speak to each other. Miss Haynes and Sister Thomas belonged to the same social class — the class of people who had been to Amurca.

Sister Thomas was the first person in our village who mentioned the names of Marcus Garvey and Harlem. At that time they were merely words, strange words.

Farther along the road, still on our right-hand side, was the Farnum family, large as a family in the Bible. They lived in a "wall house." There were six daughters and six sons. We said that the mother had children "like peas." Boys lagged around the short path to their front door. Boys waited in the dark road to count the movements of bodies behind the curtains. Boys tried to identify the passing fancy of love and breasts and daughters.

We tried to memorize the names of all the children in this family.

They had cows. So many cows that you could say they had a dairy.

Mistress Farnum used her title as a married woman with a vengeance. "Go and tell your mother," she would tell me, "that *Mistress Farnum* tell her that she'll like to have a word with her, please." The *please* at the end of the command was not added as a softener but as a small reminder of who was superior and who was inferior.

My mother was named Mistress too. But to Mistress Farnum it was a different brand; for she knew that my mother had tasted the love of man before she had worn the virgin's white of holy matrimony.

Early in the morning and late in the afternoon, I would see Mr. Farnum — a short black man, tough as herringbone, knotted and sinewed — walking at the back of a long line of cows. Following the cows, and in front of Mr. Farnum, would be goats, and behind the goats would be "sheeps."

Mr. Farnum never wore shoes, except on Sundays. In a pair of battered serge trousers rolled up above the ankles, stained with spilt milk, cowdung, goatdung and sheepdung, he would take the right-of-way from children and cars, from lorries and buses, and walk his walking capital, "money in the bank," his possessions, leaving behind the smell of cesspools and of the land.

Mr. Farnum liked his rum. And according to my mother, "too much o' *that*," meaning the cause of his many children.

At the end of the road — not because there was an end but because the respectable families lived in the middle — lived the short, well-built, brown-skinned man who knew everything about Don Bradman.

On the other side, " 'cross from we," to use my mother's term, was the shop. In addition to groceries, all your successes and failures, all your business and your secrets were "dispatched" in this shop. Credit was extended only to those with standing. Fights which brewed in the shop had to be continued outside. Women quarrelled about not being "dispatched" before someone else.

Women and men who had no jobs lingered in the shop and seemed to take all their meals there. A cheese cutter, a ham cutter or a fish cutter. The shop was opened when the owner got out of bed and closed when she was tired or had made enough money for one day, which was probably the same thing.

In the shop we saw advertisements, technicolour paintings and photographs printed on tin. The tin was always peeling. Sometimes a face or a pair of red-rouged lips would be torn apart, caught in the advertisement's deterioration. But always the message, as if through spite, would be left.

I first saw those five white girls, the Dionne sisters, in this shop. They bathed in bubbles of Palmolive soap. And everybody in the village stopped using Pears soap and other English soaps. Palmolive made you beautiful and fertile. All the women, mothers and single women who were pregnant, closed their eyes and wished for five or six children at a time as they bought "a cake o' Palmolive, please."

The shopkeeper, Miss Bryan, was a short, fat lady whose age nobody knew. And nobody dared to ask her how old she was. The men in the village said they thought she needed love, but they were warned away by her fear of God. "God is my boyfriend," she told them. She did not go to the Church of the Nazarene, which she called "revolutionary" and "too loud." She went to the more respectable and middle-class AME Church. The AME Church was larger, with walls washed in white — the colour of grandness and purity. A house washed in white paint was a symbol of something the villagers aspired to.

The AME Church had an elevated pulpit, an organ and a pastor who had a degree in theology from an Amurcan university. No one had ever heard the name of this university be-

84

fore; and no one questioned it.

Miss Bryan had a moustache. The men said she had a moustache "because she never had a man in her blasted life!" She was a virgin. One man said she was forty years old. When she laughed, which was seldom, and threw back her head in joy, you could see the fat throttles of her neck and dirt in the creases.

She was an educated woman. The older women said that in her youth she was a high school girl. "That is why she hates men so," the men said.

I would see her behind the shop counter, bobbing and weaving out of the paths of flies and bees. She slapped at them and missed them with yesterday's *Advocate*. The fat on her arm jumped and seemed about to fly off and explode.

There was only one copy of the *Advocate* on our street. It was Miss Bryan's copy. And at the end of the day, at the end of its library-book circulation, this newspaper resembled a wash cloth, dog-eared and greasy from use.

Miss Bryan kept a double-lined exercise book for her accounts. It was as dog-eared and greasy as the newspaper. The monetary history of the entire village was kept in this book, which hung from a string. The string was joined on to a short piece of lead pencil, which Miss Bryan called a "black lead." She always put the black lead into her mouth before she wrote with it.

She was a woman of means, with acres of land, some running wild, some buried in sugar canes which were not cultivated properly, some in flood water during the rainy season. She lived with her mother — Mother Bryan to all of us — whom we saw only on Sunday morning, walking with a stick to the AME Church. Mother Bryan clutched a large black leather-bound Bible, with gold-edged leaves which glistened in the sunlight and made her look more religious, a mother to us all. That is why we called her Mother Bryan.

85

FOURTEEN

I was running all over the house, closing the windows from a sudden downpour of warm rain. Through my mother's window, I saw Sister Thomas coming in my direction. As she ran, I could hear her saying, "Oh dear, oh dear, this rain. This is a night rain! Oh dear, oh dear."

By the time I got back into the front house, which is what we called the living room, she was at the door.

As I let her in, she stomped on the home-made cloth mat, looking down at the water falling at her feet; all the while blowing and saying, "Oh dear, oh dear, this rain!"

She stomped her feet, and her body and breasts moved in their rhythm. I saw her breasts jump up and down. I saw the brown flesh above her knees as she held her cotton dress in one hand and brushed the water off her legs and dress with the other. Her dress had buttons down the front, from her breasts to the tip of her petticoat which was now showing. It was faded pink, with white crocheted trimming.

She opened her pocket book and I could see the black leather-bound Bible inside, as she took out a small white handkerchief with flowers crocheted around the border. She wiped her face and smiled.

"You not going invite me to take a seat, young man? Where your mother?"

She sat down in the mahogany Morris rocking chair, and

started to rock gently to the beat of the heavy rain on the galvanized roof. She took a peppermint from a roll of white plastic and threw it into her mouth.

"Have one, eh, young man?"

My mother's rule about accepting gifts from friends and strangers was iron-clad and enforced without exception.

"Have one. Your mother won't say nothing. We're friends. Matter o' fact, I was coming to see her when this heavy rain came down. Oh dear, oh dear, you see this rain, young man?"

She stopped rocking. She seemed to be listening to the rain. Water started to drop on the floor. *Plop! plop! plop! plop!* She looked up at the ceiling, and then at the small pool gradually getting larger, like a lake.

"You won't take a peppermint from me?"

The water from the roof was falling faster. She looked up again. She got up and I thought she was going to do something about the leaking roof. But she went to the front window, raised it a little and looked outside.

"Oh dear, oh dear, this rain!"

Plop-plop! Plop-plop! Plop-plop! . . .

She sat down in the rocking chair and rocked with the rain. She brushed her dress again, rubbing her hand over it, as if she was pressing it. All the time she brushed, I could see her hand flattening her brown legs. She raised the dress farther up her legs, and I saw more of the pink and the embroidery on her petticoat. She looked up at me, and she brushed some more.

Plop-plop-plop! Plop-plop-plop! Plop-plop-plop! . . .

My heart was beating now with the drumming of the water on the floor.

"Come, look. Your mother won't mind. Look what I have for you."

She took out two peppermints.

"It's okay."

She reached out her hands to me. I saw the soft brown fatness of her arms, and as she brought me into the embrace, between her legs, with me standing at the height of her face, I caught the scent of her perfume and her perspiration mixed into one. She had a mole on the right side of her mouth, which was full, and her lips were red, although she wore no lipstick. Christians did not wear lipstick.

As I stood between her legs, she looked at me with a comforting, kind look. Her eyes were grey. And I thought they looked like a cat's.

"Take it."

My hands were occupied with unwrapping the peppermints when she held me. She dropped her hands, just dropped them, and then I heard the leaking water coming down faster . . . *plop-plopplopplop! plopplopplopplop!* . . . and I realized she was rubbing my chest, and my arms and my thighs, which reached her at the middle of the bottom of her dress. I could feel her blowing hard, like the way she was blowing and puffing when she came in from the rain. Like the way she sometimes blew when she was testifying and getting into the spirit at church.

The rain was singing now on the galvanized roof. She put more pressure on her hands and I found myself going down, down into her lap. She raised her petticoat just a little; and I saw the blue veins, like aimless worms on her fat legs above her knees. Her hands felt cool on my skin. She was saying "Oh dear, oh dear." And each time she said "Oh dear," her hands moved over my body.

The rain was beating down. I felt her hands under my shirt, and a strange sensation — like the feeling of cool water thrown over my naked body.

"You're a nice young man," she said. She was blowing and breathing faster than when she was in the spirit in the mission hall. "You is a nice little boy. You should come to church and give your soul to God. And be a Christian."

Plopplopplopplop! Plopplopplopplopplop. . .

"Open this door, boy! The rain drowning me! Open the door quick, boy!"

It was my mother.

"Well, well, well! Sister Luke!" Sister Thomas said, smiling sweetly and going to the door to help my mother with the parcels.

My mother held the parcels under her arms, trying to save them from the rain. She stood on the mat, like a soldier marching without moving, as she pounded the water out of her shoes.

Sister Thomas was smiling. "If this young man o' yours wasn't the little gentleman he is, Sister Luke, I tell you, I would be still outside in the rain, getting drown."

"I tries my best, Sister Thomas," my mother told her, obviously proud of me. "I tries my best to bring him up in the fear of the Lord."

"And a good job you're doing too, Sister Luke! Can I give him a peppermint?"

"Good afternoon, Miss Bryan, my mother ask you please hommuch she owes you, and if she doesn't owe too much, she ask to let her trust some goods till Saturday morning, if the Lord spare life, and if. . . "

Miss Bryan unrolled the dog-eared pages of her testament, her book with all the secrets of the credit of the village. She creased up her face. She turned her large eyes in more than two directions. She adjusted the non-prescription glasses with their thick lenses and brown frames. She sucked on her stubby lead pencil. She checked the items on one soiled page, in the careless wavy columns drawn by her fat fingers. Then she looked at me over the brown rims and said, "Go back and ask your mother hommuch she want to trust this time."

I ran across the road, filling up now with labourers from

the nearby sugar plantation. Their hoes and forks were on their heads, and they were stumbling tired and slow at the side of the road, walking in the gutters choked with cool grass, soothing to the feet. . . .

"My mother tell me to tell you thanks, and to ask you to please give me half pound of the fresh butter you get last week from Australia; one cake o' Palmolive and a cake o' blue soap. . . "

". . . I wonder if these blasted five girls, these quints, really born outta the same woman belly! You think that is possible? That one woman could birth five children at one time? Five? And everybody in this shop know the size of a woman's thing! It does swell and expand so big? They must have more bigger pussies up in that country where these quints come from than down here, then! Shut your ears, boy. Nobody ain't talking to you. This is big-people talk. Shut your blasted ears!"

". . . and a pint and a half o' rice. My mother ask me to ask you please to send the rice that don't have-in too much wee-bulls, not the one from Demerara. And a pint and a half o' split peas. . . "

"I didn't mek it, boy, and I didn't grow it! You tell your mother that for me! I sell what the wholesale merchants in Town send up here on a lorry."

"Demerara! That is a place and a half!" The woman who wondered about the Dionnes was talking again. "Miss Bryan, have you ever went to Demerara? Isn't it down there that they eats rattlesnakes and lizards and mountain chickens? No wonder the average Demerarian is so blasted black!"

"Not Demerara, Trinidad, man! Trinidad is famous for mountain chickens."

Miss Bryan then remembered me standing in front of her, and she turned her thick lens in my direction and smiled. She was a kind woman. Her kindness would sometimes be shown in the largest "cut-drop" in the glass case of cakes, where flies and an occasional bee buzzed. The bees made the turn-overs and the "rock cakes" sweeter. Sometimes she added an extra pig tail.

This afternoon, as she sometimes did, she tested my progress at Combermere.

"The capital of Barbados?"

"Bridgetown."

"Good. You learning good. The capital o' Inglund?"

"London."

"France."

"Paris."

"Hommany continents there is in the whirl?"

"Five."

"Wait!" It was the woman who talked about the Dionnes. She was amazed at my knowledge.

"What is the longest river in the whole whirl?" she asked me.

"Mississippi."

"Jesus Christ, boy! Where you learn all this from? You is a learning fool! Be careful that all this learning don't burst your blasted brains!"

"He young. He young," Miss Bryan said. "He is the modernt generation."

Her hand chased the flies around inside the glass case and she took out the largest "cut-drop."

"This is for you." She wrapped it in a piece of brown paper.

"Your mother cooking dry food this evening? How come you didn't mention meat? She gotta be running out o' meat 'cause the last time, according to my book, that she order meat from me was. . . " She flipped the pages, and traced back the history of our diet. "Here it is! Two days ago she had corn beef, and the day before that, salt fish. The fish-woman been round here last night, so she must be serving flying fish tonight. . . "

"Fish getting scarce, eh, Miss Bryan. Everything getting more scarcer with the war. The war hitting we hard."

91

"Wars and rumours o' wars!" Miss Bryan said. She moved heavily and very carefully among the brown crocus bags of sugar and the white bags of flour and meal, among the piled-up tins of biscuits and the boxes of aerated sweet drinks which looked like small bombs in their cases. "I was lis'ning to the BBC News and they say that so far in the war the Nazzies kill five thousand people in one day, and the British and Churchill send another six to their death. The greatest whirl leaders and whirl powers haven't invented nothing yet that could end a war. Wars and rumours o' wars!"

I stood silent as Miss Bryan offered these sentiments to the shop. Labourers and other customers filed in and listened and stood up and watched the advertisements of Palmolive and the Dionne sisters with their paint peeling off. I wished I was in Canada now, where they were born.

I turned my eyes to Charles Atlas in another advertisement, and imagined my muscles growing large and like iron; and I was chasing the boy, my competitor, from under Mistress Farnum's window, the boy who was making more progress in the smiles of the countless beautiful sisters. I painted the faces of the six Farnum sisters over those of the smiling Dionnes of Canada.

And all the time, between journeys in dreams, I could hear Miss Bryan talking about the war. I left the shop and walked across the road with the red-robed archbishops in England. . .

FIFTEEN

The cutting of the sugar canes for harvesting and grinding at the sugar factories was a time of liberty and of laughter. It coincided with the long vacation. My friends from St. Matthias who had never seen so many cane fields always came to visit me. Only two could visit at a time. And we slept together on the floor of my bedroom. We talked late into black, ghost-filled nights and woke up early in the morning and went for walks. Lots of people went for walks during the cane-cutting season. The air was fresh, the skies were clean, and lots of juicy canes were left on the cool tar roads from the previous night's journey to the factory.

We walked and sucked the sweet juicy canes and forgot about Combermere School and homework and our parents, as we ruled the empty streets with our dreams. Birds played with us. Dogs chased us. Industrious people getting water from the public standpipe waved at us; and when they weren't looking, we chased their dogs and sometimes threw stones into their ribs and made them yelp.

A policeman, still in his night uniform of black serge, comes down the shiny road towards us, ticking casually on his black three-speed Raleigh bicycle. We wave to him. And he throws his fat brown night stick in the air in our direction, in a kind friendly greeting.

"Betcha he now come from a woman house!" Johnny says.

"Betcha he was throwing dice all night and forget the time," Briggs says.

"Betcha. . . "

We walked into the middle of the island, into the middle of the morning of cocks crowing and white smoke rising from the back yards of small tidy houses; and as we stopped for breath and to pee, we could smell the green tea being boiled for breakfast and hear the island awaking. It was time to turn back.

We had walked farther than we had planned. And the road was now filled with people waiting for buses to go into Town for their Saturday shopping; and already lorries burdened with the cut canes were straining up hills, and people were calling out to the drivers, "Gimme a cane! Drop one o' them juice-nine-tray-fives for me, nuh!" And the lorries would climb the inclines in a frowned different mind and attitude.

We walked into the morning becoming hot already, and sticky; and behind us is a lorry moaning with the weight and the steepness of the hill. We are half a mile from my home, in accustomed territory. We move to the side of the road. The lorry has to change gears: go into a lower gear in order to climb the hill. It will travel at walking speed, and before it reaches the top of the hill, depending on the skill we can summon, it could be emptied of all the canes.

We know about canes, and about how they are packed on the lorry. If you pull a certain cane out from the middle of the load, all the canes could tumble out into the middle of the road.

The lorry is beside us now. We move behind it, like innocent morning walkers, and as it goes into low gear, we pounce upon it. Johnny, the biggest and strongest, pulls the "key-cane," as he calls it; and before we know it, the load tumbles out at our feet.

With less weight, the lorry speeds up, and people are shouting, and the driver is cursing, and the assistant is hopping off into the road, mad, and waving a piece of iron, the Z-shaped tool for starting the engine.

We are appalled. We knew it could happen with the "key-cane," but we had never seen it happen. So we stand up, stunned at our dexterity.

The assistant comes around to the back of the lorry, now stopped in the middle of the hill, and he raises the piece of iron over his head. His eyes are red. Cane-cutting season is rum-drinking season. And he is one of the biggest rum drinkers in the village.

"Be-Jesus Christ, if I didn't know your mother, if I didn't know you was a Cawmere boy, I would drive this piece o' iron into your fucking head, so help me God!" And for some reason, he smiles. "Now, haul all your arses and help me load back these blasted canes on this lorry! Come, come!" And he makes a feint with the piece of iron.

Sometimes we would play in the thick canes of green waves before they were cut. We were German submarines cruising for the enemy in deep waters. Attacking the British ships — which meant the man Golbourne, who tilled the land for my stepfather, and his wife, Sissie. Golbourne was a young man. And Sissie was old enough to be his mother, so the villagers said.

"I can't understand how a nice young man like Golbourne could live with a woman old enough to be his blasted mother! I wonder what he see in she?" my mother would ask.

Golbourne was the only man in the village who lived with a woman so much older than himself. We didn't know why; and none of our elders explained it to us. But Johnny, who had a special knowledge of all things, offered us an explanation. "You remember that fellow with the mother in

Amurca? Well, he have lots o' books on sex, and one day in class he was showing me this book, and now that I think of it, that book explain this thing with Golbourne and his wife. You remember, too, that in class we come across a fellow named Oedipus, the fellow who fell in love with he mother? Well, Golbourne might be really and truly Sissie child, and Sissie and Golbourne may be Oedipus and his mother!"

"Man, that can't happen," Briggs said. "It can't be the case, because Oedipus is a man in a book, and everything you come across in a book doesn't mean that you can apply it to real life. . . ."

But Golbourne and Sissie were the British ships, and we were the submarines out to sink them.

"I'm the *Grass Spree!*" Johnny said, moving silently through the canes. But the waves of the canes did not remain as silent as he wanted.

"The *Grass Spree* is a battleship, yuh idiot!"

"So what? You ever heard that they give submarines names? The *Grass Spree* is a German ship, and I is a Nazzie, so what?"

"Well, I am the *Hood* then."

"Yuh see? You must be a idiot too, 'cause you just called yourself a ship. To-besides, a British ship can't sink another British ship!"

"Well, submarines then!"

We moved through the crackling Dardanelles of canes, hoping that our progress was not noticed by the *HMS Golbourne* and the *HMS Sissie*, who were in a clearing beyond the tall waves of canes, using their hoes and forks, where my stepfather had cultivated a kitchen garden of vegetables.

When we saw them through the periscopes of the cane blades, we were going to stop, aim our torpedoes, and rush into the clearing screaming *bang-bang-bang*! and send them to the bottom.

But we could not see them. The canes were too thick. We moved slowly, stealthily, through the uncharted waters, our only means of direction being the compasses of our ears and the shaking canes beyond. They were there. Somewhere in the canes. We moved slowly, in the direction of the soft voices we began to hear. Three submarines. Against two ships. The cane blades wiped our faces like waves lashing the deck. The field was humid, the sun was hot and we were perspiring. We heard the *HMS Sissie* sighing. Something was wrong with her. She was a ship with a problem. Perhaps, Johnny said, laughing, "she taking on water. She taking on something."

Light was coming through the canes, and we knew we were getting closer to the clearing, so we stopped. The breathing continued. We could hear the *HMS Sissie* sighing, as if she was struggling. And then we heard the *HMS Golbourne*'s voice, more angry than hers, telling her something that was both a compliment and an accusation.

The light came towards us, and we stopped, and we saw them. Golbourne was lying on top of her. Her head was turned in our direction, and she was sighing. But Golbourne was not interested in her pain.

We fell to the ground, went below the surface, as if we were hit by a torpedo. We lay there, looking. We were not breathing now. We had to be quiet, for beside Golbourne was Sissie's hoe, with the sunlight making silver and lightning of its blade. And nearby, under Sissie's bare leg, was the cutlass, moving in the light and in her own movement, like a mirror.

"Oh, oh, oh, oh, ohhhhhhhhhh!"

We crawled backwards on our stomachs, hoping the trash at the bottom of the canes would remain quiet.

"Golbourne like he is a German submarine! He sinking she!" Johnny said when we were not yet out of danger.

Nobody said a word.

"The *HMS Golbourne* put one 'pon she, man! Golbourne like he is a better submarine than we, yuh!"

We walked a safe distance through the canes and came back towards them, from the *cane-brek* that began at the road, talking at the top of our voices so that they would hear us coming, and as if we had not seen them earlier.

Golbourne saw us first. He was six-foot-six. He was holding the hoe in his hand and hitting the black earth with it, as if he had something against the earth. Perspiration was pouring down his face. He wiped his forehead with the back of his hand; and he dropped the hoe. He took up the cutlass and came towards us. "Lemme cut three soft piece o' canes for you fellows."

SIXTEEN

All of a sudden people were running for their lives. They were in cars, on bicycles, and some were in donkey carts. The Germans had invaded Barbados. That was the day the man at the look-out looked through his spyglass and said he saw the periscope. The Germans had come. And life had come to a standstill.

It was a hot afternoon. A bright afternoon. An afternoon of blue skies. And the people did not think that the Germans had any business leaving Europe, or wherever it was they lived and fought and killed the British, and coming down in our waters to give us a hard time. The people did not think it was fair for the Germans to leave "all their killing and murdering" and come down into the Caribbean and bring that "sort o' lawlessness and European destruction" among us.

"They looking for a blasted war?" the men said. "Well, we could give them a fight!"

We had been content to read about the war in the *Advocate*, in the photographs in the few copies of *Life* magazine that trickled into the island, in *Movietone* newsreels at the Empire Theatre, and every night on the BBC.

This afternoon the people were running for the hills. But the hills were bare of vegetation and hiding places. They were not hilly, not high enough above the rest of the land to make good hiding places. But the hills made it easier to see the Germans in the harbour.

The Germans were coming, the men said.

In a short time, so the people said as they ran, the Germans would be landing, and the island would be put in a concentration camp. We had heard about concentration camps on the BBC.

And as in all other ways of life in the island, the people who got to the hills first were the rich people. During the war, the rich people were the white people. After the war, the black people laughed at the white people for getting to the hills first. They were "blasted cowards," the black people said. "More blasted coward than we poor people!"

Hours later on this sad day for the island, when dusk had fallen and the people thought they were safe, they said that the Germans were not going to land after all. They had just stopped by to torpedo a merchant ship, to let the poor people know that all this time during the rationing of the war, food was coming in and going out of the harbour, to be fed to those people who were "contributing to the war effort." The people said, "Them blasted Germans is really and truly our Allies!"

When the torpedo hit the ship, the whole island shook. Some people in our village who believed in the Bible said it was "the last coming." The ship which carried all this mysterious cargo of foodstuffs which we didn't eat was the *Cornwallis*.

We had protected ourselves well, we thought, from the Germans and the other *Axes*. The Harbour Police had gone out into the harbour and had placed nets in the sea. The nets were put there to catch torpedoes. But all that the nets ever did catch were fish. Dolphins and sharks. Fish was plentiful in those days. But a torpedo was bigger than any fish any fisherman had ever seen.

The German submarine fired one torpedo, and the harbour turned black. The torpedo went through the net, and all the fish which the fishermen used to pick off were killed.

For days after, the authorities moved the bowels of the *Cornwallis*, blackened and spoiled, stinking and useless, from the holds and dumped it in the middle of the neighbourhood where the poor lived.

The authorities of our country always had a sense of humour. This time they showed it in a vicious way. The food and other goods that the people could not buy were dumped in a large hole right in their back yards, now completely useless. We caught a smell of the war. And its stench. There were no rotting bodies. Only rotting cargo.

We remembered the long lists of the dead at sea that were read out at morning prayers by the headmaster in St. Matthias. And for months afterwards we played in the rot and imagined ourselves as armies and tanks of the Allies, or of the *Axes* Powers; and hundreds of boys and I picked the prizes of war from the garbage.

There were miles of rolls of theatre tickets with ADMIT ONE imprinted on them in many colours, and some men tried to use them at the Olympic Theatre and were kicked out by the bouncers; and balls of thread, and tins of canned meat from countries we had not yet met in geography classes at Combermere.

At night the more daring men among us dug deeper into the fuming wreckage and came up with a fountain pen which no longer worked, and if it did, they did not have the skill to use it. And some women, standing in fear behind the men, found pieces of cloth which they sewed into dresses with the weak, rotting thread from the same wreckage. Before the week was out, the new dresses would disclose breasts and thighs, and the women would curse.

The *Cornwallis* got itself patched up, just as the women patched up their "Cornwallis dresses" with the abandoned thread. And soon afterwards, before the stench had lifted, the *Cornwallis* limped out of the harbour.

But we were left with tales of gallantry and heroism. The man at the look-out had told me, "I was the first man in this whole island to spot the German submarine that torpedo the *Cornwallis!* Always on the job. I barely catched a glimpse of this thing peeping up above the water, and I say to myself,

'My God, a submarine, a parascope!' And *bram!* I call in my report. . . "

And a new term was added to our always-increasing lexicon. If you were hit suddenly, if you were exposed, if you had an odour, if you were not really up to scratch, you were *cornwallised*.

The hiatus of the disaster was fun for us, after the running to the hills. And one boy said, when the worst had passed, "I am going to put a blasted cornwallis on you!" Moments afterwards, his friend who did not believe him, and who probably did not understand the language, was lying panting on the warm black ground, with a blackened eye.

SEVENTEEN

The long vacation was over. The sugar canes had been harvested. We had eaten tons of roasted corn, sucked canes, and drunk "raw liquor" by the gallon. The "raw liquor" was hot cane juice. We made rolly-pollies, sugar cakes and all the native candies, and destroyed our clothes playing cricket and football and the many versions of hide-and-hoop.

It was time to be measured for the larger stiff khaki short pants and short-sleeved shirts; time to get haircuts which left our heads itching from the dull razor blades and the thick lather of blue soap and carbolic soap; time to memorize new irregular verbs in the *Latin Primer*, and the tricky French verbs; time to think of personal achievements: to be a Latin fool, a French fool, a Mathematics fool, or simply to remain a fool.

I was in the fourth form now. I was among boys who "foamed" when they peed; among boys who talked about doing things with women, not girls; among boys who talked about women in frightening whispered details — some of them already had women "in the family way." We knew that if the Major heard about this native prowess, we would be expelled.

I was emerging into that frightful time of life when, according to these boys who had women, I too could put a woman "in the family way." The thought capsized me into periods of depression: pain and regret at becoming a man so soon. To be a man meant having to work in the fields, in a rock quarry drilling measured coral stones in the hottest time of sun and sweat; meant working in the hardest of labours; being father and bread-winner to children at a time when there was little bread; hearing the shrieking voice of a wife, losing youth and shape with children born once a year; being a civil servant at a small salary for life, riding a bicycle and wearing a tie in the heat.

These stories of the older boys frightened me, and through that fear I discovered that I could be a fool of some kind. The easiest fool to be was a "running fool." An athlete.

To be an athlete was to be pure, to be concerned with health and your body. I was to begin on a campaign of fetish, with raw eggs every morning; and when my mother could afford it, the eggs were beaten in a bottle of Guinness stout, with grated nutmeg and a jigger of brandy.

I went about on my toes. I walked with a bounce off my heels, always at the ready to pounce upon a hundred-yard dash or a two-twenty; ready to run from a dog! And reminding my mother to feed me raw spinach and barely boiled beets which automatically made me strong because they left the blood-like stain on my tongue.

Blood and the colour red meant health. I would hold a finger and squeeze it, thereby stopping the circulation of blood, to show the tip of the finger almost bursting with red corpuscles.

Other boys, in love with Charles Atlas, were "pelting iron," and would emerge from the noisy clattering back yards with muscles grown overnight. I wanted to retain the body of a young Greek god. So I ran and ate almost-raw beets.

I did not become a running fool on the spur of the moment; the ability and ease to be this kind of a fool never blossomed beyond the daily sprints with dogs. It happened by accident. It was a Saturday morning.

Some of us would wander down to the playing field at

Combermere and watch the star cricketers — Vendal Babb, Moggs Forde, Pucker Marshall and Harold Brewster — young men who were destined for the Island First Eleven, and thereafter, with better preparation than my friend from the Flagstaff look-out, get a pick on the West Indies Eleven to play against England and Australia.

My responsibilities at home — looking after the sheep and the chickens and the pigs — did not leave me with enough time to practise the cover drive like Everton Weekes and Don Bradman. And after school, to play bat-and-ball in the village was impossible because I was a *Cawmere boy who had to do his lessons.* I therefore became a watcher of cricket. An applauder of cricket.

On this fateful Saturday morning, hours before the school team was to begin its match against the Police First Eleven, all of a sudden there was an elimination race for the 880 yards. The final would be run on Sports Day. And since I had nothing better to do — the clapping time for the match had not yet come, since I could only dream of the glory and pride of being applauded by the entire school for having scored a half century or having taken six wickets — I entered the elimination race. It meant going around and around the playing field, running like a fool along a line marked by the same whitewash as on the creases on the pitch. I never understood the mathematicians of our school, how they could mark the exact distance of an 880. Later on, I sometimes felt that they had given me 890 yards to run, instead of 880.

There were twenty boys in the race. A derby we called it. I was one of the youngest. The rules of athletics at Combermere were that in other events but the half-mile, you had to compete according to age. But the half-mile, the feature race of the day, and the last, could be entered by any fool so long as he had guts. I did not know if I had guts. But there was nothing yet to do on this Saturday morning. So why not be a running fool?

I stumbled around and around the uneven track, to the

cheers of the cricketers practising at the nets for their own hour of glory. I was too afraid to drop out. I closed my eyes and ran and ran, and when it was all finished, I stumbled through the tape, third! A fourth former had come third in the half-mile race, which was something of an oddity. But I should say I was big for my age.

Many mornings, riding down Bishop's Court Hill on my way to Combermere, on my black ladies' wheel, a woman would call out, "Boy, you don't know you too old to be still going school? Why don't come out and breed women?" That would make me continue to eat the raw eggs and drink them in pints of Guinness, and chew raw spinach, and admire Popeye in the comic books, and be strong for the exertions of other half-mile races.

From the day when I hit the tape third, I became a new presence at Combermere. My new status came in a dramatic manner.

It was the time for our term reports to be sent to our parents. A student whose name was John Smith would hear the master say from his elevated desk, "Smith, this report going to Mr. and Mrs. John Smith, right?" And nobody would notice.

But when he said, "Clarke, this report going to Miss Luke, right?" all the boys would want to know how it is that my name is Clarke and my mother's name is Luke! There must be some illegitimacy somewhere.

In a country where so many of us were illegitimate, each time the school reports were to be sent out there was great snickering. And at the beginning I had suffered for my mother and myself, like many other boys. We were illegitimate. Imposters. But after I hit the stiff tape *third*, all that changed. I was now a running fool, "a boy to be watched, who knows one day he may represent we at the Olympics."

The smear of illegitimacy could be erased. So, no longer was my mother's name mentioned. My name was not even mentioned. (They never mentioned my father's name.) He could have been dead so far as the school was concerned!

The master came up with a brilliant idea, a way of erasing my low caste. He did not say, as he had done many times before, "Clarke? This report going to Miss Luke?" No, the running fool needed protection from the snickers of the class.

He called me up to the elevated desk and said, "Clarke, you're a credit to this school. I'll say that Miss Luke is your guardian, all right?"

I was now not only a running fool but a fool with a guardian. The proprieties of Combermere School had succeeded in shielding me from the stigma of illegitimacy, and had placed me into the category of being a ward.

"Ma," I told her that afternoon when I got home, "did you know you are my guardian?"

"What?" she said. "What blasted foolishness they learning you down at that Cawmere place?"

EIGHTEEN

My mother loved the idea that I was a choir boy in the St. Matthias Church. And as time went by, I had the honour to sing a solo on a First Sunday and send my voice prancing all over the coral stone in the old church, hitting against the technicolour windows which showed the anger of Christ. Christ seemed angrier the brighter the sun was against the stained-glass windows.

My mother forgot her resentment about my sleeping away at my aunt's house on Friday night after choir practice. No longer did she walk the long lonely journey from Clapham to Dayrells Road, with an old black jacket thrown across her shoulders to keep out the dew, to find out "what the arse you mean" by not coming home.

So it was a day of joy when I announced that I was admitted to the choir stalls of the St. Michael Cathedral.

To be a choir boy at the Cathedral in those days was the next best thing to being in the heavenly host. Or perhaps to being an Anglican minister. The Cathedral choir boys wore purple, and ruffs, and walked slowly up the right-angled aisle with eyes half closed, looking holy as angels or priests. They carried red leather-bound *Psalters* and the blue leather-bound *Hymns Ancient and Modern*, and a book with carols and real music on five lines, minims, semi-breves, demi-semi-quavers.

It was a holy sight to see us, black boys, in red and white, black hair shining from too much grease and Brilliantine, and most of us wearing glasses because glasses meant that we were educated. All the educated people in Barbados, all the various "fools," wore glasses. They were tortoise-shell spectacles which were made in England, and which were not manufactured to accommodate the flatness and broadness of our noses. So they dropped and drooped, and made us look even more educated, like various brands of owls, like various fools.

The Cathedral was situated in Town, in the capital, and that added to its charm and importance. Everything important was in Town. The best schools were in Town. On Saturdays I went to "pictures" at the Empire Theatre, the best cinema, which was in Town.

My mother worked hard on Saturdays to get my "church clothes" ready and tidy, suitable for the Cathedral; and she did this extra work with a smile. Her son was in the Cathedral choir. It was another blessing of her labour.

She did not understand the Cathedral, the sermons they preached, the English accents of the visiting Bishops and "good preachers" (and I myself, a Cawmere boy, could seldom follow these sermons with numerous references to theology for more than half an hour). She didn't understand the hard calculus of the Cathedral's theology.

The choir boys slept and sometimes snored; the organist, who had heard more of these sermons than anyone else, nodded, and after twenty years of pumping the organ, sometimes missed the piece he played at the end of the sermon; and the congregation, even those who sat in the front pews, slept and found their heads falling off their propped shoulders, feigned attitudes of concentration.

At this time an old lady entered our lives. And when she left, we were changed people.

Miss Christopher was a woman who looked about seventy,

although if I had the arithmetic of her life, I would know she was only fifty when we met her. She passed around one Sunday afternoon about two, when we were eating dinner, and never left. Her hard life, her preoccupation with religion, her preaching until late into the night, which caused her voice to be husky, the many times she testified in church — all these demands on an already fragile body left their mark.

Sister Christopher, as she came to be addressed by the village, belonged to the Church of the Nazarene. She and Sister Thomas were church-sisters. The Church of the Nazarene was a one-room, broken-down rocking institution.

On Sundays at twelve-thirty, after I had ridden the two miles uphill from the Cathedral, the Church of the Nazarene would still be in full swing, shaking with confessions and testimonies. The tambourines and the testifying and the women getting into the spirit, milder than in Dayrells Road, would pierce the peaceful Sunday afternoon; and the cane field beside the sloping building would lean to one side, the side of the Church, and listen to the angry protests of salvation.

In the same way that schools and people and fools were categorized, so too was the Church of the Nazarene. It was slotted at the lower end of the religious ladder. Only poor people, people who had suffered, who had had the hardest of lives, who were black in a population of black people, only these worshipped at the Church of the Nazarene. It was like a political party or a business venture just getting off its feet. But it was a part of the village; and if I could have thought about it in those days of no serious social thought and awareness, it was a part of ourselves.

On the Sunday afternoon when Sister Christopher stopped by to "talk about Jesus," we had just taken the first bites of the delicious, juicy pork chops, and we were contemplating the sweet potatoes fried slightly in the gravy of the pork chops, and the dry peas and rice with generous portions of salted pig tails.

Sister Christopher knocked, was admitted and said Grace — although my mother had already commanded me to say Grace — and she took a seat at the dinner table.

In cases all around us, Sunday dinner was the only good meal of the week. Sister Christopher, who did "Christian work all week from house to house, probably knew which house had the best Sunday dinner.

"I see your son, Sister Luke. . ." she began, and did not finish until she had chewed the skin of the golden-brown pork chop. She chewed with difficulty, as she had lost most of her top teeth. "I see this boy-child o' yours every blessed Sunday on his nice bicycle going and coming from the Cathedral. I say to myself when I see him pass the Nazarene, what a lovely sight! Praise the Lord! God is in the heart of the poor and the rich. It don't matter if a boy is going to high school, or if he is like one o' them you see knocking round this place, stanning up by the road, and gambling all day long, God could still come in his heart. And I been wondering, Sister Luke, if you won't let this *fine* boy-child o' yourn pass round by the Nazarene tomorrow night, when we having a service for the young people, during our revival festival. We need some good voices in the choir. And you say this boy is a choir-boy in the Cathedral? Well, he's just the right person we looking for. . ."

It started with my mother, now Sister Luke. She was "passing round" by the Church of the Nazarene every Monday night. She wore her white dress, with a hat filled with fruits made of plastic, and native to a country with an agriculture different from ours. Grapes and peaches and some small berries that were yellow. In her hand was her large Bible. Black and leather-bound, with gold-trimmed pages and a delicate piece of silk braid as a bookmark.

"Sister Luke" would now walk across the road, cocky in her new righteousness, her face shining with the inner satisfaction of having "found God as my personal Saviour"; and she would say good evening to everyone she passed on the street. Even the most despised dweller in the village would get a nod, a smile and a greeting. "And how you this blessed evening, sister?" It was like a new political consciousness operating within my mother.

And after service she would get home just before midnight, a little frightened because of the darkness of the road; but she was not so frightened as before, because now she had God and was protected and "Christ is in my heart." He walked with her, through the strait of tall sugar canes on both sides of the road, past the marl hole, past the big gate that led into the Big House, Clapham House, past the big wooden two-storey house where nobody seemed to live, except three vicious stray dogs, and then down into the incline of Flagstaff Road, into a deep valley of fear and darkness, as she passed the only light on the street. The light was always dim. The lamp-lighter had been drunk perhaps, had had too many snaps of rum and had put off changing the bulb.

She would enter the house humming the closing hymn, and when she remembered the words, she would light up the house with her voice. She sang hymns which had beat and passion and touched her life with their lyrics.

Then it was getting down on bended knees before I could go to bed, before I could wipe my feet to shake off the day's dust from playing and running at Combermere. The Latin irregular verbs and the strange French words and pronunciation would have to wait until she "talked to Jesus."

Three times a week we got down on bended knees in a house full of strangers, all of whom said they were knitted closely together in a fellowship with Jesus. My mother had opened her house and allowed the congregation of the Church of the Nazarene to hold prayer meetings in the living room.

My Latin and French were suffering. "But Jesus, the Lamb of God, knows more Latin and more French than anybody who teaching you at Cawmere, boy. So don't you worry. The time you spend on your bended knees won't be forgotten by God, 'cause God himself would give you the answers, just as

112

he gave those men assembled in that upstairs place and who talked in tongues. God know more foreign languages than you and me, or even the headmaster of Cawmere."

Sister Luke understood Christian charity. She insisted that I attend services at the Church of the Nazarene only during the week. "You is a Cawmere boy and should belong to the Cathedral. Still. . . " and she didn't finish her thoughts. I was permitted to continue *to belong to the Cathedral*. "I myself going belong to the Nazarene, 'cause there I understand what the preacher preaching. I don't have your head for big words."

NINETEEN

The time came. It was a cool night. The cane harvest had just ended. The Sunday following was Harvest Sunday. The Church was filled. People and things. Corns, fruits, the thick-skinned speckled green-and-yellow pumpkins, eggs and food that was cooked. But tonight, Friday night, I had to have an excuse from choir practice at the Cathedral *where I belonged.* The men who talked about cricket scores and women and just plain living and the end of the war, who used to stand like cocks of the walk in front of the rum shop on the other side of the road with a jigger of rum in their hands, these men now wandered over as if they were children of Israel crossing the Red Sea, to listen, all of them meanwhile drunk, to Sister Christopher's beautiful operatic voice and witness, like the congregation of saints, men and women saved and already *washed in the precious blood of the Lamb.*

Sister Christopher took great pleasure in her enumeration of their bad, worthless lives. She held them in the palm of her voice. And sobered them up as she touched every private detail of depravity and degradation of each of their lives.

I was standing beside my mother, now a bona-fide Sister Luke. We were midway in the short row of benches, by the aisle. The hymn *Nearer My God to Thee* was being sung. Sister Christopher, who "was bringing the message tonight," had led the Church in song also. She had selected the hymn herself. She regulated the pitch of the singing. She decided how long the hymn would be sung.

114

At this time she had gone through it three times. The Church was on fire. The men and women, those who were not yet saints, who were not yet saved, were shaking. Fear; the cleansing of the Word; fatigue from a twelve-hour day hoeing, forking, cleaning the fields; sore backs and muscles from lifting barrels of molasses on the wharf in Town, and crocus bags of raw sugar, were mixed in their postures.

I saw Sister Christopher coming down the aisle. Her eyes were almost completely closed. She had the spirit in her. She needed no sight in this domain of her cruel voice. Her body was moving to the rhythm of the hymn.

> *. . . Angels to beckon me*
> *Nearer, my God, to Thee,*
> *Nearer to Thee. . .*

She pronounced each word, and saliva was spitting out of her mouth, so entranced was she by the feeling of the hymn and the feeling in the Church. She held up her hand, her eyes still closed, and stopped the singing. And she said to the Church, but really to me, "Won't you take Christ into your heart tonight, as your personal Saviour?"

It was a question which required no answer. It could have been a question whose answer she already knew. My mother gave me a slight nudge. Normally, it would have sent me staggering into the aisle, into the clutches of Sister Christopher. And Sister would have led me struggling up the aisle to the altar rail. But my hand caught the end of the pew just in time, and I diverted both their efforts to catch me, and thought the best thing to do was open my mouth wider and sing just as Sister Christopher was singing.

> *Though, like the wanderer,*
> *The sun gone down,*
> *Darkness comes over me,*
> *My rest a stone*
> *Yet in my dreams I'd be*
> *Nearer, My God, to Thee. . .*

Sister Christopher opened her eyes, although she knew whose voice was competing with hers. But she liked the competition. She wheeled around after two or three "Praise Gods" and the hymn went into the ascendency. A woman shrieked and jumped up. When she fell into the aisle, as if by pre-arrangement, Sister Christopher was on bended knees at her side, patting her on the back. The woman continued heaving as if somebody had given her a good, stiff licking with a bull-pistle whip.

Sister Christopher had caught her, and saved her. But she had me in her sights.

The hymn was now in its fifth rendition. I was getting tired. There were fifth declension substances at home to be learned for class. And irregular verbs in French to memorize. The hymn changed to *There is a Green Hill Far Away. . .*

After Sunday School, I would ride my ticking three-speed ladies' wheel, polished and oiled, along the road washed in sunlight, and quiet as a grove, quiet as Belleville Avenue, to visit my friend Kenny, who lived in Green Hill in a home surrounded by delicious avocado pears and sweet apples and mangoes.

And between bits of small talk of ambitions and universities and degrees, all of which we had already conferred on ourselves, watch with mouth-watering lust the peeled mango and my friend's sister.

Riding back, fast, with the three speeds of the bicycle ticking in one sprint, in time for Evensong and Service in the white-ruffed Cathedral, I would imagine that the road was a bower, that the canes were the vegetation of England, that the wild flowers in the clogged gutters were daffodils, that there was no difference between England — unknown to me except in pictures in English Country Life — and Barbados: for England was the same as Barbados.

There was no other good enough
To pay the price of sin

116

He only could unlock the gate
Of Heav'n and let us in.

Sister Christopher was holding my arm. I was walking, but not with my own feet; and I was mumbling. I was walking on air, in a new bounce that was more athletic than the running fool's jaunty walk, and the altar was now made out of gold, and there was silver and some gold on the wall hangings in the Church, and the voices surrounding me were like the voices of the heavenly hosts.

I was saved. I confessed my sins. I didn't have any sins to speak of, but I invented many, and admitted with Sister Christopher's urging that I was born in sin, had lived all my life in sin.

On my bended knees I admitted to sins of enormous blackness, sins of a life that was so low that to come out of this pit of degradation, my elevation would be the more dramatic and cleansing.

Sister Christopher was sweating. The singing and preaching and shouting and the Invitation had taken its wet awful-smelling toll on her body.

One minute afterwards, as I walked like one of the other Christians from the altar, shaking and in need of a good carpenter, my mother addressed me as "Brother Tom."

I had been a ward before I entered the revival meeting. Now I was even more distant from her. *Brother Tom.* I was a new man. Satan couldn't touch me. I could walk in the ways of the Lord, and cross the street in the path of a car, and nothing would happen to me. Sister Christopher told the rejoicing congregation all that the night I was saved.

And on Sunday morning I was again riding my bicycle down the two miles of safe road to sing in the choir of the Cathedral, past the Church of the Nazarene.

TWENTY

The Indian man gave us just enough time to swallow the last grain of rice, and drink the last drop of punch made of fruit juices, before he came ringing bicycle bells or honking the horn of a motor scooter in front of the house. He had come to collect the small instalments on the long-term, long-distance purchases of cheap silk materials we bought from him.

"He don't know today is the Lord's Day?" my mother always said. "He is some kind o' heathen, or some kind o' heathen?"

My mother resented the Indian man who came every Sunday. This was the tradition.

Sister Christopher had told her, "Indians have a different religion to we." They worked on Sundays, she added; and what made their work bad and sinful in a Christian place, as Sister Christopher called the entire village, was that they made money on Sundays.

But the villagers, and those who lived nearby and who "trusted" from the Indian, knew that they would hardly have time to swallow the Sunday meal before the Indian man appeared on his bicycle to collect the small payments on the never-never plan, on which everyone purchased his cheap Indian silks.

This Sunday afternoon the Indian was dressed in a short-sleeved shirt, loose-fitting brown trousers and sandals. His head was bare and looked wet, like black velvet. He was most unlike the Indians I had seen in picture books, in swamps in Trinidad and in Guyana, up to their necks in paddy fields and cow dung; or those in geography books at Combermere which showed them in their native habitat in Indian fields, walking behind zebu cows and bulls, which the books said they foolishly did not eat, and died of starvation like flies.

There were zebu cows in Barbados, and we ate them.

The bicycle this Indian rode today was new. It was green. It was made in England. It was shining. It had a tray or carrier over the back wheel. And this was laden down with a large, cheap, imitation-leather valise, from which bulged pieces of cloth of all colours and prices and silkiness. Everything about the Indian was cheap. And shiny. He was introducing us to a new economy of cheapness.

Before she met this Indian man, my mother would buy expensive English wool from the stores in Town, and spend half the year paying for it. She would give it to the tailor just in time for Christmas or Easter, to be made into my "Christmas suit." But the Indian man changed all that. He brought the cloth right to the door. She could make the purchase before she had paid a cent for it. She felt richer. But she knew she was poorer.

The Indian man charged very high interest rates. His small instalments totalled more than half the store price of the cheap Indian silk.

He would lay his bicycle on the ground near the front garden, instead of propping it against the house. With a little urging he would come into the house. My mother gave him the best chair. He would look behind him on the wall at the technicolour painting of Jesus, with a purple heart and deep-red blood coming from the heart, in carefully drawn symmetrical drops. The heart was meticulously painted *outside* the white bodice-like shirt that Jesus wore.

The silver bracelets on the Indian's hands would rattle, like snakes in children's books, and he would run his hand through his jet-black wet hair and pronounce my mother's name in a way which no one, including my mother, could understand.

119

After these formalities, he would open his bulging valise.

On most days he was accompanied by a small Indian boy. The boy lifted the heavy valise off the carrier, and his other job seemed to be to carry it into the house. The little boy's job was also to open and close the valise. Sometimes it seemed that the man was so fatigued from his Sunday money-collecting that he had to ask the boy to lift the thin pieces of cheap silk from his valise.

The haggling would take an hour, until the Indian remembered he had a whole village to take money from before the sun went down and caught him defenceless in black alien poor territory, stranded among these strange people whom he did not see on any other day but Sunday.

I would watch the Indian man and compare him to his brothers in books. His hands were delicate like a woman's. The silver bracelets on his arms were different and more precious than those my mother wore. He also wore rings, made of gold. Three on each hand. Thick black hair grew from above his fingernails, running right up to the goggle of his neck. Black hair. Silk hair. Hair like the cloth he sold.

Once he said he was thirsty. My mother offered him a glass of rum punch. He did something with his face and in his dialect, and she knew instinctively he wouldn't take the punch. He accepted a glass of water instead.

We would see him moving from house to house, like a library book circulating, like a strange, mysterious and despised man, through the classes of our village. We did not know his name, but we all called him Patel. He did not know our names, and he called my mother and all the women Madam. He did not speak to men.

I remember it once took my mother one year to pay off a purchase of four dress lengths of silk cloth. I knew when she had come to the end of her indebtedness because she declared her freedom from Patel in a strange cry of joy.

"Be-Christ! Only last January that man Patel come to my door riding a bicycle! And look! Look how Patel riding 'bout motto-scooter today! One year later!"

It had taken Patel one year of collecting small payments to move up to motorized transportation. And it had taken her the same one year to pay for four dress lengths. "I tell you, boy, if I was to go down Swan Street Monday morning, I swear to God I would see Patel selling cloth in one o' them one-door peddling stores."

And in truth, soon afterwards she did go to Swan Street — the street where the Indians kept their one-door cloth-selling businesses. And there was Patel! He was fat. He was smiling. He was dressed in Indian costume. And there were four other Indian men in the store with him.

My mother stood at the door and looked around. Angry but proud at Patel's success, which she had foretold. She came away from the sidewalk, from the incense-smelling store, no wider than a water closet but much longer and gloomy and smelling also of cloth. And she looked up at the sign above the door: PATEL AND BROTHERS.

"Christ, boy, you know which one is really Patel? The Patel we know for three years? Which one you think is Patel brother? These Indians is something, in truth! I tell you, boy, if we could eat one meal a day and save like these Indians, *Barbados would be our own!*"

TWENTY-ONE

Choir practices at the Cathedral were like drill parades. They were held on Wednesdays and on Fridays. On Wednesdays we remained in the upstairs Changing Room, which was large enough for the entire choir, the organist and the upright piano. Wednesday was the day when we became nervous and tense. And in our tenseness, we probably all became sopranos, when fear would raise our voices surprising decibels beyond the normal pitch.

A boy would be called upon to run through the scales. This would be the cause of great cawing: *caw, caw, caw, caw, caw, caw, caw, cawwwwwwww!*

"Higher pitch!" the organist would shout. "And faster!" And the cawing and lamentation would continue. Another boy would be called upon to sing the first three verses of Psalm XXIII. Another, to render the descant.

We ate crispy biscuits and did other superstitious things to enhance and make honey of our uncertain voices. Probationers in the choir were asked to sing at these Wednesday practices. And more than once, a boy with a previously beautiful voice would either wet his pants or suddenly and dramatically become a basso profundo.

It was reputation and style and showing off, and the ability to have lots of girls, that drove us into this angelic host. We wore our school uniforms during the Wednesday evening practice.

All the members of the choir were at high school, some at Combermere, some at Harrison College. In my time, no one from an elementary school, no one who did not know someone to recommend him (if he was not a high school boy), no one who did not have middle-class status, was ever a member of the Cathedral choir. We were known in Town as "Cathedral choir boys"; we were known in our villages and districts as "Cathedral choir boys"; and all the boys in the island who had ambitions to sing envied us and talked about us with suspicion as "them boys who does sing in the Cathedral choir."

You were destined to finish school culturally depraved if you did not belong to the Sea Scouts, the Number One Barbados Troop, to the cadets at Harrison College, Combermere or the Lodge School; if you did not have a rich father who sent you to school in a chauffeur-driven car, and sent back the car at lunch with your linen-napkined lunch basket and "icy-hot" thermos of warm or cold milk, then picked you up after school in the goggling awe of all the boys. If you had gone through secondary school with none of this, you might even become an overseer at a plantation, or a sanitary inspector looking for *larvees* in the dark, crawling cockroached pits of the island's privies.

And apart from that, if you were not a good cricketer or football player, you had failed, and would remain a social failure. No amount of "excellents" on your term report card could redeem you in the eyes of the "normal" boys who did all these extracurricular activities.

On Friday nights the choir practice was conducted in the choir stalls, in the dimly lit chancel. We were dressed in the black cassocks, without surplices, which were worn on certain "high" Sundays. The anthem was rehearsed until each of us knew it by note; each descant, each change.

All around us, small boys, we could smell the rum on the breaths of basses, tenors and altos, and on some of the bigger boys in the choir. The men in the choir sang alto, tenor, bass, and they drank enormous quantities of snaps of rum without ice and sometimes without water chasers, to soothe the larynxes and accelerate the notes.

Some men never looked into their books. They knew everything by heart. To know things by heart was a sign of brilliance: at Combermere and in the choir. Some would sing with their eyes closed, their heads cocked at an angle to better release the delicate notes of a dulcet alto part. Some held their lips pursed in the form normally meant to bring out a whistle, and instead a soft silk syrup of a voice would catch us and make us pause in our own parts, to listen.

The Cathedral would be dark except for that portion of the chancel where we were. And the gloom and shadows and awesome reflection of Jesus and Mary and the Crucifixion in three of the many panels of the East Window, stained in glass and metal, would make us understand our place and remember where we were.

We wore the black cassock and white surplice during Lent. But on Good Friday, only the black cassock. That was a day for having a good long breakfast to survive the long service. We sang the *Hallelulia Chorus* as if Jesus was about to come down from the stained-glass window, as if at each Station of the Cross in the large Cathedral filled to the brim, we expected to receive a hand of congratulation from him. And many of us fainted before the sad liturgy was over. It was not an embarrassment. There was no shame. We had, in our remembrance of sorrow on earth centuries ago, succumbed to the long watch merely because we were frail.

Some of us had probably not got home before midnight the night before. We might have been at a dance in the Queen's Park shed; visiting our girl friends — those of us who were *mannish* enough to have girl friends. We might have burned our candles at both ends, and didn't get enough sleep. *Could ye not watch with me, once brief hour?* It had a meaning for some of us, like a double flogging.

At St. Matthias Church the choir was good. Not as good as the Cathedral's, but more relaxed. The men in the choir there had an island-wide reputation for singing. The best tenor in the island, Humphrey Walcott, was at St. Matthias. The best bass singer at the Cathedral. And sometimes a man from one choir would come to another's church and sit in the Sunday-night Evensong congregation like a spy, to settle for himself and his backers the competition and arguments about reputation.

My voice was trained at St. Matthias. I learned Roman numerals; how to find the services for the various Sundays; *Septuagessima; The Magnificat;* the *Collects;* the Sundays in *Advent* and in *Epiphany;* and there too I decided which hymns I liked best.

At St. Matthias too I learned how to stand for the singing of a psalm which I could not find because of the Roman numerals, and watch the mouth of the head boy, and open my mouth and sing without a word coming out: *caw-caw-caw-caw*ing all the time, because where I sat my face was a close-up in the mirror the organist kept above the pumping keys. That ability to sing without knowing the words followed me throughout choirs and schools.

But one day I met the head boy and he invited me to climb over the wall of the church. We found ourselves in the choir stalls, amongst the smell of church and incense and black cassocks, whose presence were left there through the ages. We jumped on the organ keys, planks of wood, and played Bach and Purcell and somebody named Palestrina, and nothing but our two voices came out. *Gloria in Excelsis!*

The head boy ordered me to go behind the organ and find the wooden shaft, the lever, the "pump," and move it up and down, and put breath into the bowels of the voiceless organ. And soon afterwards, holding onto the "pump" like the fan of a windmill, all the basso profundos, arpeggios and "rah-luh-tans," crescendos, everything bellowed and lifted the church and me on the climbing "pump" of its feet, in the glory and excitement of excelsis of our unskilled hands.

As I went up and down with the pump, I remembered how on some Sundays the organist's face would turn red and we would think we had missed a note, later to find that the assistant sexton, whose job it was to "pump" the organ, had fallen asleep from the snaps of rum he had snapped to keep him awake during a long Good Friday service.

Then we bowed, as we would every Sunday before leaving the sacred chancel, and walked silently down the long aisle in our bare feet. We stood at the West Gate and bowed again, and bowed a third time, and hummed the organ piece which Mr. Williams always played as the choir walked out. Then the head boy, who had no work this afternoon, no gainful employment, and who lived nearby, said *The Magnificat* as if he was an Englishman, and made the sign of the Cross just as the vicar, an Englishman, used to do, as if he was chasing flies from his face. The head boy held my hand and we walked into an office which smelled of silver and old cloth and wine.

He did something to the keyhole with an object in his hand. He took out the large crystal decanter with the deep-red liquid in it, and held it over my mouth. "In the name of the Father, the Son and the Holy Ghost," he said, just like the English vicar, "confess your sins, my son, and you shall enter the kingdom of everlasting life. . . " He lifted the decanter over his head and tried to say the same words for himself as he drank. But he almost choked. Wine ran down his lips, like blood. He held the decanter at his bloodied lips until he had drunk half of the rich, strange wine. We were, neither of us, "confirmed" Christians before he blessed himself.

It was a Monday afternoon. No meetings or services were held in the church on Mondays. It was quiet and serene and frightening. It was the first time I was in a church with only two persons. We had passed the assistant sexton in a rum shop in the village, where he was arguing about who was the best woman contralto in the whole island — for this church, unlike the Cathedral, had women in the choir.

"What you think the vicar does-do with the wine after he serve Communion?"

I shook my head.

"I uses to wonder myself what he does-do with all the wine the people don't drink at the rails. But when I became head boy, he called me in here one Sunday after church and ask me to sit down. He take the big silver cup off this same table, with the white cloth on it, and he ask me to go outside for a glass o' water. When I come back in, he and me put some water in the silver cup and stir it round in his hand and he put it to his head. When he take that silver cup from his head, his eyes turned bright and his face turned red as a cherry. He ask me if I does-drink, and I tell him no, I don't drink."

Before we left, the head boy ran his hands over the white linen cloth on the table on which was a shining brass cross. The linen cloth had a cross crocheted into it. He touched all the silver cups of various sizes and put them back in a straight line. He ran his fingers over the surplices of the vicar's, over his Bible, and over the crimson collection bags made of cloth with a gold embroidered cross on each. He lifted the lid of one of the collection bags, and in the thick furry pouch was a brown penny. He took the penny and put it in his pocket.

"This is a coconut bread," he said.

Back outside in the brilliant sun of the dying day, my face began to get big and my head was like the black bird on the steeple of green ivy. We passed the assistant sexton. The head boy told him, "My mother say she bringing the choir robes for the choir tomorrow morning, hear?"

"Look, boy, buy me a nip-bottle o' rum, if you coming back out here. Mek it a nip o' Mount Gay." He gave him a shilling. "Keep the change."

We rolled across the road, whiter now in the last sun of the day, and dusty from donkey carts and the few cars which passed us, hands wrapped around each other's neck in a choking embrace of friendship, walking like two sailors we had seen off an English ship, from side to side, like the waves, *"drunk as two Nicodemons."*

If you were drunk in our village, you did not only totter, for that would be without style: you had to do more. Everything around us had style. If you were drunk, you had to sing. So we loosened the necktie of riddled boyish guilt that joined us in love and secrecy, and we sang *For He's a Jolly Good Fellow. . .* The head boy sang the tenor, and I carried the rocking bass line.

TWENTY-TWO

Suddenly one morning I opened the top half of the window in my bedroom and looked outside into the awakening bedrooms and windows of the village, windows that looked like large unpainted eyelids; then over the tops of the houses nearby, over the tops of the sugar canes, and over the miles of cruel green fields of various shades of green, patched like a quilt, where the men had forked and where the women had driven the sharp hoe into the savage black soil; over the arrangement of the land by the sugar plantation: house and clump of fruitless fruit trees nearby, giving shade and dignity; over the farther tops of ripening sugar canes, with the silk "arrows" on them, making them into a large sea with foam and waves, barely moving.

I opened the window with a ruler. It was like an awning, and it was like a large eyelid. The houses nearby and far were already drenched in sunlight. They were painted in as many colours as their owners had whims. They had names: *Labour Blest. In God We Trust. The Cottage. Flagstaff Castle.* Even the most dilapidated, shingled by flattened tin cans picked up out of the garbage, carried insurance against fire, hurricane, flood and storm. And in the most conspicuous place above the front door, they had nailed a rusting shield with the word *Royal* barely visible.

I looked out this morning onto all this brightness, this

harsh seven o'clock sunlight, and I could see that the plantation house was visible only in parts, where the trees did not swallow it completely from view. I looked again at the houses, chattel houses, as we called them, some with one roof, some with two, and not many with more than three; houses painted red and green and blue and grey, and various tints of those colours. Never one painted white! I looked again at the hidden plantation house. And I saw that the first man in the village, dependent as the entire village was dependent on the plantation, which was our symbol in the many ways of our lives and our ambition, this first man must have looked as I was looking now, out into that first morning, after he had accumulated two boards and a half-pound of nails and a sheet of galvanize to build this one-roofed chattel house, and then had *seen the similarity!*

He must have seen that the plantation house was hidden in part from him; and using the house close up when he was in its yard milking the cows, taking out the manure and the cow dung, or sweeping the plantation yard, he must have seen the model for his own house. He saw the luscious trees covering part of the magnificent plantation house. And he copied exactly that portion which he could see, and which he could afford.

And that is why the chattel house is merely a section of the plantation house — that part clearly visible in the morning sunlight. It was his only model. And it was the blueprint of his perspective, drawn in the hazy distance of many evenings of dreams and many mornings of blinding ambition.

In St. Matthias village there was no plantation and no plantation house. Only the Marine Hotel. There were no fields of green, and no silken arrows like waves. There was always the dust of streets carved out by our feet toughened from the stones in the road, and the various alleys and lanes, charted through impulse and necessity, through the mud and drier parts of the area where we lived.

Out the front road were the drug store and big houses with paved roads. The houses were washed in white, with high white-washed walls, and gates which were locked or latched and carried the signs *Beware of Dog* or *Trespassers Will Be Prosecuted.* Some of the walls were washed in pink.

I would walk these streets out the front road just after noon, when the sun was hottest and most cruel, when the stomach was emptiest. We had "tea," which was anything from a cup of green tea to a large meal cooked at five o'clock in the morning, or else warmed-over food from the previous night.

At noon the stomach was empty and growling. Barefooted, I walked these streets in the memorable afternoons, with a dangerous grumbling stomach. It was always during the week after we were "dismissed" from school, so I was barefooted. Shoes were bought to wear to church or school or the General Hospital to visit a sick relative. The streets could be so hot, and so soft from the heat, that I would often leave my footprints in the black macadam.

When I got to the end of St. Matthias Gap, I would stand for a while and watch the drug store. The large bottles of glass that contained "sweets" and medicines and pills of all sorts of toughness and strength and sweetness.

I could see the drug-store man in his white jacket, like a surgeon "dispatching" a customer, and behind his head was the blue sea. I could smell the contents of those bottles even from that distance. Lysol was the main smell that came from his dispensary. All the large bottles had Latin written on them.

The drug store stood on a hill. If I turned left, there were more houses, built some distance from the road — through the architecture and planning and respectability; and guarded by high, washed walls with the signs *Beware of Dog* and *Trespassers Will Be Prosecuted.* And always a small wicket gate where you had to stoop and bend almost in half to get through.

Servants and beggars entered through this gate, which had a bell nailed inside. You touched the gate and the bell alarmed the dog and the owners. And you left in haste, with no message or money, because we believed the dogs out the front road were taught to eat black boys alive.

On the side of the sea, silver and blinding and at rest, was the Hastings Rocks, an esplanade with a gazebo in which the Police Band played hymns and marches and calypsoes with indistinct beats for the white people.

Now, minutes after noon, while the men are eating lunch in the cool large gloomy dining rooms, the nannies dressed in starched white are on the paved Rocks, sitting on green-painted benches or walking in circles, wheeling white children in huge perambulators. The sea breeze and the sprays which escape above the breakwater lull the nannies and the children and the dogs to sleep.

The afternoons would be white and hot and clean and still; and empty. The gutters would run with clear water, no green moss here, as in the gutters on our side of the front road. And I would walk to the end of the Hastings Rocks, turn back and go farther in the opposite direction, from the Gap which led to the "back," to St. Matthias Village, where the poor people lived.

The sea was louder in this section of the walk.

Down the hill of coconut trees, tall as the roofs of red and silver galvanize. In the darkened drawing rooms that faced the road, I would see the sea providing always the background for a head or a body that moves quickly and becomes a shadow; and hear the murmur of the waves deep below.

On the side away from the sea was the huge Married Women's Quarters, stone and brick painted red, with green shutters, like large eyelids, always on the point of falling asleep. And clean roads, and quiet; and trees shading the nanny sitting on the root of the evergreen tree, with the child in the huge pram. The trees in this front road section were hard and stern: mahogany trees, mastic trees, fustic trees, cedars and, of course, bearded fig trees.

The Married Women's Quarters used to house the noncommissioned officers of the Boer War, the old people said. And at church on the first Sunday of the month, we would see some of the remnants of that time when the British Colonial Army camped among these hard trees. They came with the "soldiers" and the pipe band of the Barbados Volunteer Force, which marched like Tipperary in straight lines of khaki and precision along the Sunday streets.

Those who lived in the section near the Rocks came too. At the end of the service, the poor people waited with their hands on the backs of pews as these relics of another time crept from their pews at the front of the church, slower now through age and illness and the declining weight of their wealth. We watched them hobble out into an easier spiritual forgiveness; and within five minutes they went from us like needles and camels in a haystack.

A man, blackened by the sun and the relentless heat, comes towards me, pedalling in low gear on a bicycle. He is dressed in khaki from head to ankle. Around his ankles are two black bicycle clips. He wears no shoes, and his feet cover the delicate rubber pedal like a wicket-keeper's glove covers the hand. On his head is a hat made out of cork, the colour of khaki, with green undersides. He sweats and looks grim. There is no definition on his face; only resentment and fatigue; the pain and hardship of his employment. His face is set against showing any emotion. Never a blush or a twitch. He would not dare to smile in my presence because he is "on business," on white man's business, perhaps on His Majesty's Service and business. His eyes are almost closed as he pedals against the steady incline of the road, but you can glimpse the redness in his eyes.

There are rum shops on the way from Town, and he has stopped for a "fiver" and a snap. He writhes from side to side, his neck moving like the head of a turtle.

The street is empty. And clean. I step from the surface of the melting hot road and stand on the cement slab which is a footpath built over the gutter running free, with no green moss, and no fish heads. I look down on the hot tar road and see the prints left by my feet. I dip my feet in the water of the gutter, and I feel the relief. And I think of walking on the beach, leaving larger footprints in the sand. I think of Robinson Crusoe whom I read about in books which do not say definitely that Barbados is the island on which he landed. But we believe Robinson Crusoe lived here.

On the way to Town there is a piece of brass on the side of a house which says *George Washington Slept Here*, and we believe that, and can tell you with whom he slept and for how long, and what he left screaming for a bottle.

I think of Friday. And of course no teacher, no master, has told me yet the other meaning of this man Friday. No one, not even the brightest schoolmaster in the island, knows what Friday stands for. He was only a footprint, one teacher said, a footprint on the sands of time. I always liked the way he put it. *Footprints on the sands of time.* I was a footprint on the sands of time. Many times. And so were my friends. And my mother and stepfather.

The war was still on. I was sure the war was on because of the quiet in the whole land. And the sun was hot. It was still after midday. Five hours away from the next meal.

Where was my mother at this hot time? She could be in a kitchen, in any one of the kitchens of houses I am passing now; or in the ironing room, running the hot slab of iron, held with a burnt cloth over the rich sea-island cottons and the cottons of the rich.

Where was my stepfather? He was also in the broiling sun at the training school for police cadets, learning how to turn right, and turn left, and slope arms, and present arms; and how to write a report in a small black notebook with a small polished mahogany-like pencil with a white plastic tip on it. An elastic band round the book held all his newly learned "procedures" about the Law. He walked with this book in the back pocket of his uniform trousers.

I was walking now on the slabs of cement laid out in the

134

pattern of a hopscotch; over the clear running water in the gutters; and soon I would reach the section in the wall through which I could slip, a natural wicket gate, and jump from stone to stone, going down the hill with the giant coconut trees, through sea-grape trees and almond trees.

You never saw a grape that was ripe. They were all eaten before they could reach that stage. Other boys had come here before me. But if it was too high above the head, an almond may be ripe for a boy with a stick, or a jumping boy to "lick down," or a boy on another's shoulder to "lick at."

And then the beach. Gravesend Beach. The tombstones are sunk into the sand. And the grey crabs and the blue crabs and transparent crabs run here and there, like insects. And there are insects too. Invisible. You know they are there after they have stung you.

The trees do not let the sun through, and your hunger is soothed and there is the shade to loll in; and you are cooled by the sea. Here and there a man with a black cloth around his loins, shining from the sea water and from his obsession with the body beautiful, stands like a monument, like a tomb, like Lord Nelson in the Town square. He is up to his waist in the sea; and he holds a white net in his hands. He looks at something at his buried feet and does not move. And when he sees it — his dinner — he flings the net, which looks like a speeding cloud too close to the water; he miscalculates and the cloud of net is gone. He has missed. He has lost his dinner.

Later on I see him drawing up his net, dripping with water and pieces of silver which are frays and sprats, and sometimes a larger fish caught napping in the shallow waters.

I do not speak to this fisher of the sea. He is like a king of the deep, and all the water within sight is his.

I walk down the beach, dragging my feet in the wet sand, kicking a dead crab out of my way, avoiding the cobblers and broken shells of sea eggs eaten in haste, raw, against the law, for the law says you cannot eat sea eggs in any month of the year that does not contain, in its three-syllabled spelling, the letter "r." But all of us have eaten sea eggs in the month of *Aurgust*!

The tide is out. I walk far into the sea, on the slimy blackened iron pipe, seeing things I have never seen before. And I know when to end my precarious walk. At some distance, there are welks and sea-beefs; and if I am lucky, a sea egg left without kith and kin, or escaped from the fisherman now buried to his neck in the coming waves that hit against his chest and then disappear with his dinner in them.

I can see footprints on the sands of time. And I stand on the black pipe, sucking the rows from the shell of the sea egg. There is no one but the fisherman and me. I am Tom here; or Austin Ardinel Chesterfield Clarke, a Cawmere boy, a running fool. And I think of a line in a poem, written about a boy I do not know and may never meet, on this beach or elsewhere, who *stood in his shoes and he wondered, he wondered; he stood in his shoes and he wondered. . .*

TWENTY-THREE

When I was promoted to the fifth form, I had never passed an examination in French (*je suit, tu suis* was not enough to conduct the three paragraphs of conversational French in which the Major took us!); and I had never passed in trigonometry (simple equations was the high point of my mathematical genius).

In these days I was dreaming more than I had ever dreamed before. The white hot road out the front road, and the plantation house; the Battle of Hastings; 1066 and all that; other pieces of English history and culture and English civilization which were my daily intellectual fare at Combermere — all this stuck in my mind and I lived in this Union-Jacked time as if I were in an English countryside.

I was a "dreaming fool," and my dreams found me writing poetry. They were copies of English poetry. What other poetry would I know? Milton and Keats. Milton was always dear to me because in my new village my best friend was named Milton. Milton, the friend from St. Matthias, had moved on from watering the roses in the Marine Hotel to the hold of a ship that one day stopped in the harbour, and when they found him, he was in America. Something happened, and they did not send him back. But he wrote us once from a place called Chattanooga, and signed his name "Hank." We had always thought that Chattanooga was a place in a song, a place along a railway line, a place where they shined shoes.

One evening as we were pulling up the thick-leaved pawn grass to feed our sheep and rabbits, I asked this new Milton whether his name was real or a nickname. How could someone so close to me, someone I saw walking barefoot every day, with holes in his trousers and the smell of sheep on his shirt, how could he be named Milton, like that blind man who talked about paradise?

"Were you really christened 'Milton,' Milton?"

"They just christen me so," he said, and nothing more.

When he reached nineteen he moved away to father a child from a woman who already had three from three different men. The woman was wise and beautiful, and cruel. She joined the church. And he had "seen God," he said.

His stepmother was Sister Thomas of the Church of the Nazarene. Before I was "saved" by Sister Christopher, Sister Thomas had left for Amurca through the help of a cousin. It was soon after the day of the heavy rains, when she offered me the two peppermints. Had she not left, I would even now have been like Milton, *walking in the name of the Lord*, even before Sister Christopher seduced me to the altar.

"She start coming round the place," Milton said one evening when we were sheltering from a sudden downpour, under a large eddoe leaf. "She start coming round. One Sunday. And then the next Sunday after church. And Miss Thomas would put a plate o' food in front of her. The biggest plate o' food in the house. Not that I did mind Miss Thomas giving she more than me or my brother. But Miss Thomas would take half of my meat and half of my brother meat, and put it on her plate with the most of the food. She could sing good in the choir too. And Miss Thomas, before she went away to Amurca, had saved her. Man, it was the only time I went near she. It was only one time. One time it happen. Right there by that eddoe plant, in the part that we clear way last year to sit down under and talk 'bout things and life. We only do the thing one time. And the

138

next month she tell me that she in the family way and she going have to tell Miss Thomas. So she tell Miss Thomas, and Miss Thomas saved she. Miss Thomas tell she, 'Child, even if you was my own daughter, I won't want no fatherless child in my home. I going get you saved quick and turn you into a Christian.' So Miss Thomas saved she. She fool Miss Thomas, but she didn't fool me. 'Cause as I tell you over and over again, I intend to be a motto-car mechanic. And no woman that I got a child from, or say I got a child from, can stand in the way of my becoming just that. A motto-car mechanic."

But Miss Thomas saw it otherwise. She was a strong pillar in the Church and a stronger pillar in her home, both of which had suffered heavily during the last rain storm. She did "save" the young woman. It was during a harvest festival too, before the harvest when I walked the plank of salvation.

"I don't want no sinners living under my roof," Miss Thomas told Milton. And she made him and his brother kneel down along with the woman, on bare knees on the floor which always had sand to help keep it clean, and pray and confess. Milton said he confessed to sins he never committed (I thought of Sister Christopher). "I made she happy by confessing to some sins I didn't even know was invented," he said. "My brother confess too! We invented sins like peas."

It did not matter to Sister Thomas that the four bakes, which was all the family of four sometimes had for dinner during the lean months after the Allies won the war, now had to be divided into five and soon into six. Milton resented this division; he was a German-lover and a follower of Himmler.

It did not matter that Milton and his brother had to sleep in the shed-roof, the part of the house where the cooking and socializing were done. Sister Thomas was a better Samaritan than the one about whom she preached so fiercely on Sundays. She made a bed for her "precious daughter-in-law" on the floor of her own bedroom, which she shared with her iron-fisted husband, where she could listen to the gentle snores of the woman four months pregnant, with a child being formed in her belly three months before Milton said he had even seen her.

"You safe in here. In your condition in here, no man can't lay a finger on you," Milton told me Miss Thomas said. "And you, Milton, you going walk this earth regretting till your dying day this terrible deed, this unwanted seed that you have lay on this poor, precious young child."

Milton said the woman slept on the bedroom floor for months, until the night when he was ordered to get a hundred buckets of water from the public standpipe and his step-father was ordered to dig a small hole at the back of the house. His stepmother bathed first in water with bush leaves in it, changed into her white dress, put on a makeshift nurses' cap, and brought the crying, slimy child from between the woman's legs into this world. Milton said he peeped through a hole where he had seen rats travel, from the front room to the shed-roof, and saw the whole thing.

"It's a girl!" Miss Thomas had said with a sigh of relief and great victory. It was the first time she had delivered a child. Milton said she fell on her knees and prayed for fifteen minutes; and in her nearness to God, she almost forgot to do certain other sanitary things demanded of a new birth.

Milton was ordered to bury the "birth." He covered it over with damp mould and stomped on it as if it were a centipede, to make it flat like there was nothing buried there, flat like the rest of the mould in the back yard. It was beside the tall luscious pawpaw tree that he buried the "birth." From that day, Milton said, he never ate pawpaws.

Three generations now lived in the small, weather-coloured house. Sister Thomas preached a long sermon on her victory, and on the salvation of the young woman.

One Sunday after Church, just as Sister Thomas crossed her threshold and took off the shiny black high-heeled shoes she had got from her "cousin" in Amurca, she called out to the young woman to put the supper on the table. Every meal

140

in Sister Thomas' household was called supper. As she was still humming the last verse of the closing hymn — *Just as I Am Without One Plea* — she called out again to the young woman who was not only daughter-in-law but also maid and cook . . . and heard no answer.

The spirit moved Sister Thomas, Milton said, and laughed as he related the story in the pawn grass under the broad eddoe leaf. "Miss Thomas call out again, and the spirit moved her, and she got up and went inside her bedroom, and just before she pull back the blind, 'cause the bedroom don't have no real door, just as Miss Thomas hand touch the blind, she hear a heavy breathing in the bedroom. She pull back the blind some more, hard. And right there in front of her, on the bed, was my father laying down 'pon top of the girl. . . "

Milton didn't talk for days afterwards. He was silent. And he would murmur things which I mistook for poetry. "Set your affection on things above," was one of his sayings. Then he would drop into a cold silence. Sometimes he said things I mistook for verses of hymns, which he had learned in the Church of the Nazarene when he was a "brother," before he had sinned.

Milton stopped talking to his father. This was not a strange occurrence in the village. Many fathers did not speak to their children. They would convey messages and orders through the mother or the woman who lived in the house with them. Milton started walking about all day and night, and he stopped picking pawn grass for the animals at home.

One evening he casually mentioned the blood all over the house — on the china in the polished mahogany cabinet which was opened only on Feast days, Easter and Christmas, and which only the visiting pastor could use. He said something about all the plates being smashed, and the three mahogany chairs, plus the Morris chair where Miss Thomas, almost two hundred pounds now, sat reading her Bible every morning and night; and he talked about the blood again.

Sister Thomas left soon afterwards for Amurca.

The last sermon she preached to a packed church — for by now all the villagers had heard of the scandal — was based on the text, *Deliver me, Lord, from the hands of the Egyptians.*

And Milton, through some strange love for the girl, through his deep hatred for his father, and perhaps because he loved his stepmother and was now lost without her on his nineteenth birthday, when he was "a man," he moved away from the village and set up house with the woman in a distant country village at the other end of the island.

His father remained alone in the small house, which was always shut down and never painted again, except by the natural hand of the heavy rains and the sun and wind blowing across from the plantation house. The postman said the front window was never opened more than twice a year, when he delivered a birthday card and a Christmas card from Sister Thomas, who was now Reverend Sister Parris.

TWENTY-FOUR

During the war water was scarce. The people were told it was scarce because the Germans had poisoned the water. And the "soldiers" from the Barbados Volunteer Force rushed to the reservoir with guns and bayonets, to guard the water.

"Water scarce as shite," the people complained. "Water shortages," the authorities announced, "will continue as a wartime measure."

People would line up at the pipe in single file for yards and wait for the dripping tap to fill their buckets. Some brought buckets that held one gallon, that held half a gallon, that had holes in them. Sometimes they were so angry that they had to wait so long for a bucket to be half filled that they walked away, cursing the authorities. And in their rage at life and at the authorities, they sometimes threw the water away in the road.

A splash would hit the stones and pebbles on the gravel road, and a few drops would settle on a woman's foot. You could see the water making her skin darker, two circles on the ashen foot.

You would hear the rattle of the galvanized bucket, hysterical like a woman's voice, and the thud of another one, and all of a sudden the line would break and there would be shouts and screams, and braided pigtails of the women's hair flying in the wind. Two women would start ripping each other's clothes. The woman whose foot got the two dark dots of water would scream and rush at the one who had wasted it.

"You blasted so-warrior! You blasted black so-warrior!"

She reaches now for the woman's hair and tugs on it, and her hand slips off the freshly braided hair and falls on the woman's chest, near her breasts. The hands grab the dress, that part of the thin laundered-and-worn dress where her breasts are. And the hands tighten onto that part, and soon two beautiful, ripe, full-grown "bubbies" fall out of their homemade cradle.

The few men in the line gasp. Then there is silence. The men are seeing a sweetness which they had only imagined for years as this big-bodied woman passed them on the street or brushed against them in the narrow doorway of the shop. The shop on the opposite side from the pipe empties as if there is a fire. The men look and in their minds make love to the breasts and wish the fight would never end.

The other woman, thinner but stronger, and with a reputation as a warrior, holds onto the woman's neck, and they tear at each other as they wobble about the road. And then they fall to the ground in the marl and gravel, in the few small pools of discarded water.

The men cheer. And then the real fighting begins. Their dresses are ripped to threads. Parts cover their heads. And the men can see. Everything.

The small boys remain in the line because this is "big people's business," but they know that no custom in the village says they cannot look.

So we look, and we wonder: *we stand in our shoes and we wonder*; and make comparisons, and feel ashamed to be witnesses to this terrible grown-up exposure of two women's private parts. We had talked about it for years, but only the most daring and privileged among us had seen it — those who had been seduced by older women, usually maids and servants. At Combermere there was a boy who bragged that his

father ordered and overseered and congratulated his perform-
ance with the maid. He told us, "My father does get a piece
offa she too!"

Now at the height of the day, in the blazing sun, on this
short stretch of gravel road, a circle is formed. And in the
middle are these two women. Both of them are old enough
to have children, and in fact there are seven children between
them. The men do not raise a hand to separate them.

Custom in the village says they must be impartial and not
interfere — even if a woman is their wife or "woman." I
always felt that a man made this custom. The men could see
in public what they had yearned after in private. And it was
almost the same with the boys, who could not take their
eyes off the beauty and shame and sensuality.

The women are still rolling on the ground. There is blood.
"Blood!" somebody shouts. And there is moaning. "You
bitch!" There is almost complete nakedness now. "You
double-bitch!" And as they roll, we can hear pieces of sentences about personal habits of sex, bits of secrets about
lives, and the first-hand knowledge of men who had secretly
fathered children in the village.

They tire themselves out without more damage. A dress is
destroyed. A head of African hair looks bristled in its disarray.
In their bareness, they look at each other and dare themselves
to stop. One woman tries in vain to make a net out of her
dress to hide one heavy black bubby. She sees the men staring
at her, and she screams, "Look, look! But not one o' wunnuh
is good enough to touch!" The men drop their eyes and stand
foolishly, moving their stubby large toes in the gravel road.

The other woman adjusts her dress like a harness, holds
her breasts in her hands, one in each, and with a shrug makes
them fall into the loose space between her dress and petticoat.

We drift off, leaving them to make the most of their knowledge of each other, and as witnesses to deeds which curdled
the blood and left our young minds confused.

This is the history and civilization of our village: this

sudden cruel exposure of secrets which only the old people know, and which has kept the village knitted together in a close simple love.

I think of Milton and his child, who was his brother; and I think of Sister Thomas somewhere far from this screaming noise, in a country, Amurca, where according to our textbooks at Combermere and the other Milton who sometimes wrote us, noise could be even louder, and where blood flowed in rivers.

And before the day was over, before the last chicken jumped up on its roost, I saw the same two women walking side by side, sharing the grains of a roasted corn.

TWENTY-FIVE

Years and years and years ago, when trains and tramlines used to run in Barbados, before the day they stopped, a day nobody remembered as a date in history since there was no such measurement of time, I remembered something which happened to me when I was one year old. I told this to my friend Kenny one afternoon as we sat in class listening to the Latin master translate Vergil, *The Aeneid*, Book One. The master was Sleepy Smith, whom we dubbed "The One and Only." He was translating as if he was an Anglican minister reading the *Collect: I sing of arms and a hero, who first sailed from the shores of. . .*

"I remember something that happened to me when I was one year old," I whispered to Kenny. Sleepy hated whispering in class.

Kenny took his eyes off the Latin master, who had by now reached *Italiam fato profugus Lavinaque venit litora.* Kenny knew the translation by heart. I depended on him in times of stalled brilliance.

"Scientifically speaking," he said, "that is impossible."

Kenny read strange scientific magazines and scientific comic books which his mother sent to him from Amurca. Kenny was born in Amurca. He wore large brown brogues with lots of holes in the shoes, brightly coloured shirts (on weekends), and his pockets were always full of ball-point pens in colours from red to yellow and green.

Once he got a pen from his mother which we all had to touch and write with. This pen looked like silver, and had at least five colours and five ball-points, one for every day of school. We were forbidden to use ball-point pens at Combermere, but we used them anyhow, especially to write love letters to the girls at St. Michael's Girls' School and Queen's College.

"Anything that a person remembers before the age o' reason is unrational," Kenny said. He had shown me a book, *The Age of Reason*, which he said he read on the bus from Town to Green Hill. He spoke like an Amurcan and had his heart on Amurca. He said that after the examination he was going back to Amurca to become either a scientist or a doctor. "But lemme hear what you propound," he said.

"I remember one morning, I think it was before school because people were still at the standpipe in Dayrells Road getting water, and the first 'Progressive Bus' didn't gone back to Town yet. A lotta people were in the road, going to the pipe and the shop.

"I remember all of a sudden my mother pulling me from my father. She was holding my head and my father was holding my feet. My father didn't like my mother, and my mother didn't like my father. . . "

Musa, mihi causas memora, quo numine laeso. . .

"And you should have heard the people screaming! 'Oh shite, Gladys, you going brekkoff the boy's foot? Oh shite, Packard, you going kill the boy? And you don't even pay child-money!' And that is all I remember. But I remember the important thing, the fight. Hours after that, I woke up with a bottle of milk in my mouth. . . "

. . .tantaene animus caelestibus irae?

"In the culture of tribalism. . . " Kenny said. He had lent me some of the strange scientific books his mother sent him from Amurca. Every month she sent a barrel, and buried at the bottom with the chewing gum were the scientific books. "In certain tribalistic societies, the members of the tribe decide matters of the highest legalistic points on the spur of

148

the moment. But take a place like the United States of A. There, the Supreme Court would take years to settle that similar problem. Paternity rights have taken a nose dive to maternity rights." When he finished the sentence, I thought the world had come to an end. I had never heard him talk like this.

The Latin master was still translating. He looked up, caught Kenny's lips moving and asked him to translate: *Urbs antiqua fuit. . .*

In our long private conversations I could not always understand what Kenny was saying, but it was interesting. I liked his Amurcan accent. It was pleasanter than the English accents all around me. And Kenny never let you forget that he was an Amurcan! Combermere School was like a summer camp to him, he told me.

He finished the translation and wanted to do more. But Sleepy was democratic and he wanted to divide the burden equally on our unenlightened shoulders. Another boy, Rochester, staggered through the translation.

I was still at the "culture of tribalism" and the United States of Amurca when Rochester reached line 32. Kenny was breathing hard. He suffered from asthma. He took a deep breath, filled his lungs with the breeze that was sweeping across the playing field, then he squirted something from an L-shaped bottle into his mouth.

We all admired him for this, and we squirted the bottle in our mouths, and we wanted to suffer from asthma with Kenny. For we loved him. But the L-shaped thing he used was from Amurca. Our moral support would have to end there. When he was breathing regularly again, he said, "I am that too. A bastard. But I am an Amurcan."

I owned very few of the textbooks we used at Combermere. "The war," my mother used to say with a sigh, as if the war was the hot afternoon. "The war, the war, boy."

The war meant that I had to sit down in an empty classroom, as many other boys did, and copy every line from the

149

original of Vergil, *The Aeneid*, Book One. We had learned at St. Matthias that *practise makes perfect.*

When I reached the fourth form against the expectations of all the masters who taught me, I spent the first month of the long vacation copying out the textbooks I would be using in the new term. We copied Vergil and Livy, Book XXI, which some boys said was the "hardest piece o' Latin in the whirl"; and one boy even copied out the *Acts of the Apostles.* We wondered where he came from, for there were more Bibles in Barbados than all the fish in the Caribbean Sea. I copied out the *Merchant of Venice.* I once felt sorry for Shylock. It was like a simple extension of association by plight.

Whenever I was in a plight, of small or large significance, I was an Israelite. We all pitied the plight of the children of Israel. The Israelites! A word of cryptic tragedy and poetry. We had never seen them, but they had crossed the Red Sea and our imaginations, and had got themselves disentangled from the bonds of Egypt.

In my entire schooling in the island, nobody hinted that if I was going to be partial to and identify with a foreign racial group, it should be because of the logic of my own ancestry, *not* the Israelites but the Egyptians.

But in Sunday School we had already been taught to dislike the Egyptians. They had put people in bondage. Shylock was therefore a reputable man. He knew about bondage. I cried with him and was moved to tears by his speech about blood and justice and bondage: his justice became my own justice against the authorities, against the assistant masters at Combermere, against the British Major, who could never be Shylock.

Everything I knew about the Egyptians came from books of adventure and mystery: they were shown on horses with long knives in their hands. But Shylock was a small man, a brilliant man, an illegitimate man, who broke bondages and stuck his finger in the laws and regulations that surrounded his bondage; and he showed their flaws.

Sister Christopher used to break down the shaky altar rail

150

and scream and say she was positive she would break out of her bondage.

Bondage came to mean a hard examination or a bad headache, or too much housework given to me by my mother.

For days and days we copied out our texts, and then we tried to learn them by heart. We improved our memorization of Latin by using a Key. A Key was the key to all things. Some masters who were not too capable with the more difficult constructions of Latin verse, some who had not prepared the lesson, and others who had read it years ago and couldn't be bothered to revise — all these ran headlong into the embrace of a Key. All except Sleepy Smith. Sleepy was our genius, our gentle hero. Oratory with Latin translation, with the Key under the desk, became our sign of great intelligence.

"One thing about living in Amurca," Kenny would tell me, "anything you want and desire, you can get. And if they don't have it, they would make it for you, or fake it. Or send away for it." So he asked his mother to send him two Keys. He kept one and sold the other to a master who was studying for his Intermediate Degree to the BA General (External) of London University, by correspondence. The Key came in handy for this brilliant scholar-to-be.

"You have to have the Key," Kenny said. "Give me the Key, Churchill told his Eton Latin master one day, and I will open the vault of Voltaire. He passeth not in Latin."

When we had copied out the Latin texts, we turned to the Latin grammar. We enjoyed doing it, although it was hard work. We did not think that to have to copy out all these texts was a sign of our inherent poverty, or even a statement of our deprivation. We thought it was caused by the war and by the authorities. We were Combermere boys. And the boys of Combermere could do no wrong; could do anything, even copy out the entire *Acts of the Apostles*. It was good for our education.

TWENTY-SIX

I chose the Cadet Corps. Perhaps it is more correct to say the Cadet Corps chose me. No, I chose the Cadet Corps. I was tired of wearing the uniform of the 23rd Barbados Scout Troop, in which I was troop leader. There was not much space left on my uniform for badges: badges of merit and badges of demerit.

I solved the question of badges and space by finding a Cadet Corps uniform that fitted me. I was attracted to this new uniform. And to the possibility of wearing a gun on my left shoulder. And marching all over the island and into the country districts, during the "crop season" of sugar cane, in big black boots with cleats in them, and singing *It's a Long Way to Tipperary*. On the way back from these marches I used to see armies of cadets coming down the road, happy, important, the Pied Pipers of Hamelin, with every girl out in the street, as they sang *John Brown's Body. . .*

To be a cadet meant you had glamour and girls. And it meant getting off a little early from classes, a half hour perhaps, on Wednesdays, when you could *clunk* your desk top and announce in a casual way, "Cadets, sir."

And all the boys whose eyes could not see the translation of the Unseen would wish they were cadets. And the master would raise an eyebrow, knowing that he had half an hour more with an Unseen, which in some cases he couldn't himself translate, and wish that the damn bell would ring the steamy afternoon to an end.

"Cadets, sir!" I would go out with a swagger to drill and pretend that in time I could be a general or a Caribbean dictator.

When you joined the cadets, if there wasn't a civil servant in your background, if there was not an English Prefect car or a Rover or a Humber in your background, if you did not live in a "wall-house," you were usually given the rank of "acting lance private." It was not necessarily a joke! Before you could be a private, you had to "pass" through a few lower levels.

I was a running fool when I chose the cadets over the scouts. So I automatically became a lance corporal when I joined. There were no tests and no courses in weaponry. There was no weaponry. Kenny joined with me, to keep me company. He was made a lance corporal too. So we marched about, even on parades on the Garrison Savannah when the Queen (or the King) was supposed to be there and couldn't come, and when the Governor of the island took the salute with rifles made from thick pieces of board fashioned by the school carpenter. Only the corporals and sergeants and the sergeant-major, the highest rank a Combermere cadet could reach, only these ranks had the weighty privilege and military honour of holding a rifle that was not made by the school carpenter. They used old .303's. The bigger boys who were not in the Cadet Corps laughed and said that these .303's were used by the British in the Boer War. They had their firing pins ripped out. So we, who may have resembled the enemies of the Boers, could not injure ourselves with these relics.

As our models for military discipline, we had the English, whom we saw each time we went to the Empire Theatre. They would stand like "mockmen" in front of Buckingham Palace, and not even a fly could make them blink. And we had the Barbados Police Force, not yet "Royal," and the Barbados Volunteer Force, not yet an "army," both of whom were imitating the English.

We did not like the Americans for military precision drill. "Amurcans can't drill like the English," Kenny had to admit.

He was happy in the Cadet Corps. Latin was becoming a bore, he said. Precision drilling was the only superiority of the English over the Amurcans that Kenny ever admitted. "When you talk 'bout the *Royal-salute-preeee-sent-arrrms!* and right turn and left turn and about-turn, well you gotta hand it to the English. They invent it!"

We despised the Amurcans also because they chewed gum. We despised the Amurcans because we were English. Colonial, overseas and overseered English. For in our history books, the English had fought the greatest battles of all time. The wars of the Roses. The Battle of Bannockburn. What a beautiful title for a battle! The Battle of Hastings, 1066, and all that. The Battle of Trafalgar. The Spanish Armada. What had Amurca done for us in its history books to make the "world a safe place for democracy"?

We English, colonial, overseas and dominion to the spit and polish of our spine, had looked down the muzzles of our board rifles on the Amurcans. The only things we heard in history about the Amurcans were slaves. Men who walked about with banjos on their knees, singing and saying Yes'M and No'sM, and Yassir and Nasser, and possum and pissum.

My great-great-great-great-grandfathers, my grandmother told me, "didn't really slaves, yuh know, son. They was kings. You is a King too." Her maiden name was King. We were Kings, four generations back in the darkness. We were not even descended from those Amurcan slaves, my grandmother told me.

No history book at St. Matthias or at Combermere dealt with this shameful Amurcan invention. It was the Amurcan blacks who were slaves, not the English blacks! England would never allow any of her subjects to be held as slaves. It was therefore far, far, far, far back in a past, which we had brushed clean, that there were slaves to be found, not related to us. That is why we despised the Amurcans.

Amurca had slaves; Amurca invented slaves; Amurca oppressed black people and turned them into slaves; Amurca lynched black people and killed them as slaves.

Kenny was the first Amurcan I knew. It was Kenny who told me these things about Amurca, and told about a secret order of men who wore white sheets with crosses instead of shirts and pants like everybody else in town. "Them's the Ku Klux Klan!" he said. We laughed at the stupid name for a secret order.

So we carried the guns made by the school carpenter, and the .303's from the Boer War, ready to fight the Amurcans or anyone who wanted to pick a quarrel with us, and dare tell us there were English slaves in our grandmothers' blood.

We staged mock battles. Mock camps. Mock enemies. We fired our mock guns at mock planes. Dropped mock hand grenades on the Germans and Amurcans in our imagination.

But more than anything else it was the glamour of the uniforms and the shining brass attachments that called upon our bravery and patriotism. For all it took to be promoted from acting lance corporal to sergeant, or even to sergeant-major, was that you had outlived all the other boys. If you didn't catch a cold, if you didn't have an accident, if you didn't have to spend a long vacation in the General Hospital with typhoid fever, if your pass marks were good, you found yourself one morning with three stripes on your shoulder.

Form by form: rank by rank, in the Combermere Cadet Corps. And you had the chance of swapping the gun made by the school carpenter for a gun used in the Boer War, with its firing pin ripped out in your interest and safety. Perhaps it was ripped out in case you as a colonial overseas and dominion type of person, unaccustomed to wars and "rumours of wars" and battles and roses, might shoot yourself and cause the authorities the expense of a postmortem examination.

You picked up a few tricks in the Cadet Corps. When you were in the fourth form you could not be a private. You knew too much Latin and French to be an ordinary private. To be a sergeant, to lead a line of "men," to stand at attention in the savage sun and watch the Governor take the

Royal Salute for the Queen, who regretted she could not be present, you had to know some Latin. There might be a chance that you would have to convey a very important dispatch to the Queen herself; and how would it look if you did not know *amo, amas, amat, amamus, amatis?*

At Combermere School we could not be cadet officers, could not be promoted to the rank of second lieutenant, because our education stopped at the Senior Cambridge School Certificate Examination, Overseas, Dominion and Colonial. It was for the "other" boys, at Harrison College, whose education ended with the Higher Certificate of Education, Oxford University or Cambridge or both. Those boys knew three more pips of Latin, and Greek too, so that they might talk to monks and priests and become doctors and barristers-at-law, and be equerries to the Queen, and be exempted from the first year's examinations at Oxford and Cambridge. Those "other" fellows could be officers. We were second grade; they were first grade.

On Speech Day we lined up in front of the school, like rulers. Not moving a muscle even when the rain came down and changed the stiff khaki into plastic, and made the brass buttons dull and like lead, and changed the white-blancoed belts into thick milky watercolours.

We didn't move a muscle. Flies were prevalent on those hot afternoons. We did not move. Our parents looked at us proudly and pointed us out to strangers, also parents, and said, "God bless." We did not move. The Major, without his pips and decorations, watched us and said, "God save the Queen!" and probably thought of his own days in Africa.

We did not move. A fly would light on our bottom lip, and we could think and remember epidemics and plagues and typhoid fever. Still, we did not move. The fly had earlier stopped to play on the garbage in the canal at the end of the playing field, and might have frolicked on the piles and lines of horse and donkey manure, like land-mines in the street, marking the journey of the Governor from his mansion at

Government House, right to the spot where he stands now. We did not move.

A fly might even have licked the sugar cakes in the nut-seller's tray, "Toffees, yuh nuts, sugar cakes, comforts are nice! Look muh here! You want me, young fellow?" And when she was caught napping, the fly might have helped himself with her sweets; might just have been a sanitary inspector, working as a sanitary inspector in the toilet just before it landed on our lips.

We did not move. We refused to move a muscle. We were at attention. The Governor was inspecting the ranks of his Guard of Honour. And we were all English, overseas, colonial and dominion. How could we move? No one, in the long history of Guards of Honour and of Combermere, had ever moved a muscle when the Governor was looking.

Some of us fell to the ground through sunstroke. Some of us fainted because we were standing too long on empty bellies, and an army marches on its belly. Some of us caught colds which grew worse and doubled up with triple-pneumonia; we'd cough and spit blood, as if we had consumption, that unmentionable tubercular disease. Some of us broke wind just as the Governor passed. Our muscles had grown too weak and our stomachs empty. But still we didn't move.

And when it was over, and the Governor left in his horse and buggy with the Union Jack licking cork in the breeze, and he travelled back to Government House along the same dots and dashes of horse manure, older and drier and with more flies, we rushed into the school canteen and savaged the ginger beer and buns, rationed to us on this day by the Queen. Benches and chairs fell before us like the Germans. Privates and acting lance corporals and lance corporals were rationed one bun and one bottle of ginger beer; corporals and sergeants got two each; and the sergeant-major got three, according to some regulations made in the commotion.

The officers who were masters rushed to the Common Room and drank rum and ate corn beef and onions and pepper sauce. But in the canteen, among ourselves, we did not see the wisdom and justice in dividing food according to rank. For food had always been shared according to appetite and size. If you were big, you got the lion's share.

There were some privates in the Cadet Corps who weighed two hundred pounds. And left to his own weight and greasy, angry avoirdupois, no sergeant-major in his right mind, even if he were loyal to the regulations of the Queen, would dare to carry out those regulations of the Queen and share according to rank.

The Queen was safe and sound in Buckingham Palace, and the Governor in Government House sipping Scotch and soda.

But this was Combermere, a school beside a canal, in the hot tropics of temporary standards, where people fought for water. So who was so colonial as to suggest that according to rank, so shall it be to appetite?

At Combermere sometimes smallness and thinness and sickliness, and of course wearing glasses, meant you were brilliant. I did not know many large, big-boned athletic boys who were considered brilliant, or at least were treated as such by the masters. You had to look sickly. You had to look as if you hardly ate, as if you spent all day in a darkened corner, grey, and all night over a kerosene lamp with a paper shade, poring over knowledge to make you into a Latin fool, a Mathematics fool, an educated fool.

Those of us who wanted to succeed forced ourselves to be stunted, small and short. The most brilliant barrister-at-law in the country was short. All the officers in the Cadet Corps *at that place*, Harrison College, were short. It seemed you had to be small, sickly and wear thick horn-rimmed glasses to be taken seriously. And of course a father or uncle in the civil service was a great help. A head teacher at an elementary school, a lawyer or a doctor, and you were assumed to be like father. You had to have class to succeed at Combermere. Brains played second fiddle.

You were "important" at Combermere if your family owned a wholesale grocery, if somebody with your name was a big lawyer in Town, if there was a manager of a sugar plantation in your bones; if you were "light-skin," which meant you had wealth, you were somebody.

If you qualified in some of these ways, you could have children from as many women as you liked. Their colour and class did not matter. The women could agree or be forced to lie down under you, and you could breed them, those blacker women.

You paid them back with the supreme compliment of allowing their children to use your name. It was a "good" name. And these children suddenly became "somebody with good name." They may never have seen their fathers. They may never be invited to their fathers' businesses along Roe-buck Street or down by the wharf, or into their fathers' homes, where a cold wife watched like an eagle. But they had his name. And his name was gold. The name was known throughout the land, and in other lands, and sometimes over-seas, colonial and dominion. The name was powerful. You had that name, and you were powerful too. And your colour did not matter. You were Mr. So-and-So's little boy.

No assistant master who wanted to get promoted, to be able to get the authorities to put electricity into his house, or the Department of Communications and Works to run the main pipe a little farther along his line of row-and-rotting houses, no one in his right mind who understood the politics of politics would give such an "important" little boy a hard time in school. This little "important fool" could even move from form to form without having passed an examination. He would find himself floating along with the rising tide, like cork, licking cork, floating along the gutter water of the front road. He would rise with the tide of patronage.

159

TWENTY-SEVEN

She was a tall strong woman even when I entered Combermere. She was a black woman, a big-boned woman, a woman who walked with her Bible. She dressed in clothes which could not be identified as to colour or shape or fashion. She was too old for fashion. Clean clothes, nevertheless. But too many skirts, too many blouses, too many dresses for the brutalizing sun.

She was of the time when women covered their sickliness under layers of dresses. An old woman.

She was sixty or seventy, could even have been eighty, when I entered Combermere. I could never tell her age. And I could not ask because we were taught to ask no questions hear no lies! And to ask your mother or father or aunt, or anyone older than yourself, his age was a petition of rudeness. *Dogs amongst doctors!* But she could have been much younger, although she looked ravaged by life and the war.

She was a daughter of a system of a time of mornings and evenings of hard work. A daughter who may have known where in Africa her father's father's father and mother's mother's mother's mother, and certainly her own mother, had come from. She knew of the May Dust that came from St. Vincent in 19-something and whitened Barbados in ash. She knew of Queen Victoria. She still carried the shining shilling which Queen Victoria, bless her kind majestic heart, made certain every subject of hers, in the colonies, dominions and territories beyond the seas, and in India too, received on her Jubilee. She knew of times when trains and trams ran in Barbados; and of the times after that, when they stopped running. And she would say to me, as older persons said to misbehaving children, "You won't have no manners because when you born the train was done running."

In her younger days she would not have been a school teacher. She did not have the chance to spend time in school. She would not have been a seamstress and made dresses for the rich, because she could not have afforded the sewing machine and cloth, perhaps bought from Indians circulating the villages even then. She was a maid, or a washer of clothes, or a servant: someone who went through the wicket gates out the front road where the signs read *Beware of Dog.* She would certainly have worked like a slave, even though she may not have been one.

Yes, she would have worked like a slave, for as she got older her back began to bend. But it might have been bent even when she was a young woman and had to stoop over the long ironing table with the slab of hot iron, or over the "jucking board" to wash clothes for her family and the mistresses and masters out the front road.

But now she was retired. No work to go to. Tired all over again from the memories of those days. She did not spend these workless hours in her small house on a hill along a gravel road.

She would walk to each of the homes in which she had worked and knock on the wicket gate and rattle the bell to be let in. "How you today?" she would ask the mistress. "Well, God bless." Then she would leave or be asked to leave, with a slice of bread from yesterday's breakfast, given to her at the request of the mistress, as Queen Victoria had given her head on a shilling.

She must have smiled with the present servant and known that soon she too would be making this journey to visit her former mistress.

Sometimes she would get a paper bag of steamed rice, plain

white rice, cooked for the diabetics. Sometimes a shilling. Sometimes, I am sure, she would look into the garbage, because she remembered when she was a young maid she would put her "take" there, in those pails and bins, and at the end of her period would walk proudly through the wicket gate, without a blemish on her character, with nothing that did not belong to her.

When she worked as a scrubber of floors at the Marine Hotel, the watchman searched her, searched her stiff petticoat and felt that young soft body, and asked her a question of availability and willingness. So she would have to remember. She would understand, for the sake of her own moral protection and her protection from the policeman who would be summoned, that her take had to be taken off the premises and hidden in the garbage.

This morning she would make her "tea" and move through the gravel road, saying good morning to her friends. She ignored her enemies, gave them "a look-off" but uttered no threat or abuse, because the trickiness of poor life had already taught her how easily today's enemies could be tomorrow's friends. The supply of food in the village was tricky, and it changed from hand to hand with impeccable swiftness.

She would walk in the bright sunlight, over the scorching road covered with small stones and marl, until she came to the church. St. Matthias Church, where she was christened. And if she was ever married, she would have been married in this church. Her children would have been christened here. She would know the vicar and the sexton.

She would enter the church now and say a short, silent something on her knees, to her God. And while bent in prayer on her ragged knees, she would remember even the words in the Bible, *manna from heaven*; and wish, through the miracles the poor have always believed in, that some token would land in her basket before she had walked too many miles.

Her basket was her home. Her basket was her bank account. And she would rise from the pew, a pew at the back of the

162

church, for she knew her place even in an empty church, and walk out into the sunlight and say "God bless" to the sexton watering the flowers in the church yard, and sprinkling some of the graves of the neighbouring rich.

She passes the school now. St. Matthias Boys' School. While I was still there, I would lift my head from the arithmetic book and catch a glimpse of her moving over the school yard, in mud, in dirt, in dust, in various seasons, and wait with my breath held in to hear the headmaster say, "Clarke, your grandmother!" All the boys would laugh; and I would be tempted to pretend that I was not Clarke, that she was not my grandmother, that I was not alive.

But the headmaster loved my grandmother, and he would not let me hide. This old woman who travelled miles in sun or rain to bring her "little gran-gran" a biscuit, a half of a slice of coconut bread, because "we living in a war, in some turrble Godless times, Mister Headmaster."

Now she moved on to the corner, facing the drug store, whose owner knew her.

"If I didn't have respect and love for your grandmother, boy, since the time me and her went to school, I would really call a police for your ass and lock you up! You coming in here looking like you want to steal! You disrespeckking your grandmother, boy!"

The candy she gave me could have come from him. It was English candy wrapped in fine white paper, with an inside wrapping and a strange smell of cleanliness, like the sea and the homes of the rich.

Turn left and walk along to the Hastings Rocks and see younger versions of herself with English prams carrying English children; versions dressed in starched white, in starched black with white caps and white aprons. "How things, daughter? I so-so."

Farther along, along the clean sanitary front road to her first wicket gate with *Beware of Dog* and the bell on a small iron spring. *Tinga-ling-ting!* Nobody home. And by the time she reaches Town, walking at her own rate of determination and love, it would be after two in the afternoon.

Her feet are either hardened or sweating. The road is tar. The sun is hot. Her hair, turning more green than grey, shows slightly under her hat. On her forehead and around her ears is the perspiration of the foolish and the poor. She is that man in the poem "Resolution and Independence."

I do not know if she has eaten since she had "tea." I do not know how many insults she has had to live through in this journey. I do not know how often she has fallen down in the middle of the road, and how many cars have had to stop an inch from crushing her head, from running over her brittle body. I do not know how many other times she has been taken to the Casualty at the hospital because of "bad-feels." I know of one time. There must have been others, for she walks this constitutional every day but Sunday.

Once she took in with badfeels in the headmaster's office and had to have smelling salts put to her nose to kick life back into her slipping senses.

She would come to my form room and tap on the door and say, "Please, sir, I come to see my gran-gran."

And the boys would laugh.

"And who is your grand?" the master asked her the first time.

She moved right inside the door, brushing past him, and came among the giggling middle-class boys, this old woman like a slow-moving ball of rags, and put her accusing finger on my shoulder, and hugged me and kissed me with her wet lips and smiled, showing no teeth at all. "This!" she said. "This is my gran. A wonderful gran he is. God bless him. And God bless you too, sir."

The class could not continue after that. I was bathed in the ridicule of my colleagues, all except Kenny who *knew*; bathed in their smiles and conspiracy; buried in shame that I, the running fool of Combermere School, was connected to this bone, this root, this poor old woman.

She saw only love, not pride. Soon after this, her visits

became a part of the school's timetable. Boys would tell me, "I saw your grandmother in Town. She coming up here." And the masters would say, perhaps because they had such a reference in their private past and present, "Your grandmother coming through the gate. If you feel ashamed, go out and meet her."

This old, pure, beautiful woman. Bent beyond all medical belief and help; walking in the hottest of suns with her basket to give, from among the trophies there, her only "gran-gran" a glasseye, a comfort, a paper bag of cold diabetes rice. And when she didn't have the luck of an answered bell, a kiss with her wet lips.

Before she died she told me she was going to die. "Soon, I won't be visiting you no more, bothering you. Getting old, you know? The body tired. But you is a man now. I glad I live to see you make such progress. God going protect yuh, even if I don't see my way to visit yuh no more. God bless."

Her life faded as her words. And after some time, all of a sudden we realized she would not be visiting us anymore. But we all remembered her. And loved her.

For years afterwards, the boys who grew up with me would put me on guard against some danger by saying, "Tom! Look, yuh gran'mother coming through the gate!"

Her name was Miriam.

Miriam amo.

TWENTY-EIGHT

Belleville Avenue was the ironical showpiece of my country: clean and white, clean and black. Riding the ladies' wheel to and from Combermere, Belleville was a street to be avoided after the sun went down behind the green fences of tall trees around the Belleville Tennis Club on its west side.

Belleville was the centre of tales and rumours told to us miles away in Dayrells Road, and afterwards in Clapham. But Clapham found me more fortunate and moving up the tricky social world of Barbados. By the time I reached Clapham, Belleville had changed and I was changing.

But in my younger days, in the days of Belleville's glory, when it still possessed its colonial charm, and rumours of terrible tales, many of us ran from its streets after dark. Punctually at five the road sweeper would appear with his rolled-up trousers, efficient as a starved dog in a gutter, and in a fast rhythm walk with his broom whose fibres were like teeth, sharpened to gnash at the smallest speck of dirt and garbage and bird shit along the slowly moving running gutters.

Belleville was a street where you strolled with a purpose, and with no idea of loitering on your face. A place that sent you back in dreams and in the pages of history printed in the old *Advocate* newspapers, to a time when coachmen dressed like fat cockroaches drove the wealthy in the lazy afternoons.

The mile trees on this avenue, if they could talk, would tell you of the grandeur of this place. They could also tell you of the happenings: of the black hands that kept the lawns looking like the tops of billiard tables; that scrubbed and polished with sand and blue soap the armoury of kitchen and bedroom utensils, pots and pans and chamber pots, making them shine like silver and china; of black hands that changed diapers, ironed shirts, slapped white bottoms; and in many cases, that brought on white orgasms through love or through rape.

Belleville was the place against which we measured our misery, and our mobility.

It was beyond the maddest dreams to imagine you could live on Belleville with these nameless rich. It was foreign territory. The names of the people who lived there were like the names of people you had read about in a book of history: people who were dead. But like the pages of history, they could not always be understood, although you had to believe in them. For believing was a part of your education.

So you would walk up from Combermere, and if you were not too hinged to the snobbery of being a Cawmere boy, you would dare to walk through Carrington's Village, where the poor were packed like jam and sardines, and feel that you were not the poorest in the land. And as you emerged, walking over rocks along these lanes, you thought only of the flood and of the great names that had come out of this area.

Carrington's Village was a place left and forgotten, and remembered just in time after it was flooded and washed away. And when the storms came, almost every year at the same time, the people who lived there were left to drift down into the Constitution River; and after a few days, three as the Bible would have it, these abandoned people moved back to the place where they were born, for it was the only home they knew.

So you left Carrington's Village with the slime of poverty, left the people living in the castles of their skins, and you stood facing the black policeman in his stiff parade uniform, a silver strap under his chin, standing at ease with a rifle that fired blanks at parades and live ammunition in riots, guarding the gate of the Governor's House, and guarding the Governor,

167

colonial, overseas and dominion. And if you were lucky, you would see the policeman snap to attention as a man in the back of a car came through. That would have been the Governor.

You knew that the dogs in the streets behind Government House did not want you to pass their way, so you chose Belleville instead, a lesser peril. You did not choose Belleville because the dogs were less ferocious; you chose it because you knew there would be a woman selling flying fish, her hawking voice not calling out too loud, as she raised it in the poorer districts; or the bread man pushing his unloaded cart, heavier now that it was emptier, after the accumulation of walked miles and sold cut-drops and floats and turn-overs and flies compounded by two smells: his and his bread.

On Belleville Avenue a maid, a nurse, sometimes even the gardener, would turn their faces when you passed. You did not belong to the same social class as they. In all the years that would remain to you, in all the years they would remain among the armoury of pots and pans and chamber pots, of their times with orgasms, with the slapped white bottoms, they knew that you would never pass any examination big enough to land you beside them. So they despised you. You were like Amurcans to them. You would get a greeting only if your mother worked in a house on this avenue.

So you walked a silent journey, not noticed by the black woman in the black uniform with the white cuffs and white cap. You kept your eye on the road. You kept your other eye on the dog lying at the maid's feet. When the dog got bored with kissing her black feet, it amused itself by jumping over the low paling and putting an L in the bottom of your school uniform. And you knew, from times past, that the maid would have to defend the mistress' and the master's testimony. It would be her way of defending her job. And her job meant her children's food and perhaps their school uniforms at Combermere.

Everyone who belonged there, by right or by labour, was well fed and quiet, as the big-bellied lazy dogs which lolled in the love of their fortunes.

No buses passed along this avenue. Who would be catching them? The maids would walk to work; and at night, in the purer darkness, they hopped on their men's bicycles and were taken silently across the low-gear road.

One afternoon Mickey and I walked from Combermere, arguing furiously about cricket.

"Don Bradman can't be the best crick-crick-cricketer in the whirl!" I was disagreeing with the man at the look-out. "What happen to the three W's — Walcott, Worrell and Weekes?"

And the people of Carrington's Village joined in our argument. We stood among them for a few minutes as they straightened out arguments with a rigid eye to history, without even raising their eyes from the board on which they slammed the dominoes. For them cricket was the only thing that could cut across social barriers.

The moment we reached Belleville, we walked without shouting. With hushed voices, we passed each mile tree.

We were on bicycles at another time, and as we reached Belleville, we got off and walked across the avenue. Something in the ticking might upset the dog, the master or the maid. *Dogs amongst doctors!* We walked to school and sweated two times a day, or rode and sweated. But each time we walked across Belleville, we didn't perspire.

But one afternoon Mickey broke wind. He closed his eyes immediately as he heard the explosion. He had been telling me about mathematics, for he was a Mathematics fool. I saw him open his eyes, and then he did the strangest thing. He said, "Excuse!"

Belleville had the power to overpower us. It made us do strange things when we found ourselves along its magnificent avenues. And we walked along it as if it wasn't a part of our lives. But in a strange way, stranger than the avenue itself, we knew it was ours, an important part of our growing up.

We might one day have it for our use, or for our misuse, as a means of comparing our poverty with its magnificence.

We had it as a means of escaping the rundown gravel roads of Carrington's Village. We had it always as a reference point.

And if there were ever any among us who could dare to dream in those grand terms, in Belleville's terms, then we had it to conquer.

I was now in the fifth form — the time for nervousness and seriousness; for long nights working out the logic of Latin irregular verbs; for memorizing whole chapters of the "Axe of the 'Postles." It was the time for learning the capitals of countries, their vegetation, "cool temperate oceanic, on the west coasts of large land masses"; their fruits, whether deciduous or otherwise; for remembering all that Goot Webster taught us in his dramatic geography classes.

I had succeeded in writing out the entire text of Vergil, *The Aeneid*, Book Two, and I had learned the translation by heart. There was no point in knowing the meaning of each word when you could sing it like Sleepy Smith: *I sing of arms and a hero, who first sailed from the shores of. . .*

Sleepy had taught us to be a Latin fool, to walk as he walked in his cut-down brown Army boots. He had taught us manners and had taught us to be ambitious.

Sleepy was the first black man I knew who was an officer in the Army, in the Volunteer Force. And he wore his pips like the pips of success, like a master — with pride and dignity, and as an example, like a Latin fool.

Before he left, he told us that he was going "up" and that it would be Law. "Law, boys! The Law! Yuh can't guh wrong with that!"

We were dreaming dreams of reality: they could come to pass. One among us had done it, and he told us we could do it too; some of us would do it better than he, he told us. "Some o' wunnuh better!" He was that honest, Sleepy was. He gave us a real education in the Latin we learned to sing like him. And he taught us who we were. We were prepared. Perhaps he was preparing us this time to get accustomed to Belleville Avenue!

170

TWENTY-NINE

My stepfather was prospering. All of a sudden on Saturday afternoons a donkey cart with a tired sweating man sitting "cat-a-corner" on the seat would arrive at the house and deliver three pieces of lumber.

My mother would come out to the front of the house, like a new bride. She would raise her voice to alert the neighbours to her growing fortune, give the donkey a good slap of thanks and its driver instructions about handling the lumber, which was placed under the cellar.

Before the driver left, he got lemonade in a glass with a saucer, and before he had left, the same instructions were repeated more than three times. The three pieces of board had been bought with the price of blood. My stepfather had passed the necessary examinations and was now admitted to the Barbados Police Force.

In those days policemen lived in barracks, and he would be away most of the week, except on his day off. His barracks were the Central Police Station in Town, beside the cells and the law courts.

In the meantime, the lumber was being accumulated, piece by piece, and the house would soon be big and fit for a young man who went to Cawmere to study in for the Cambridge School Certificate and afterwards the Wolsey Hall correspondence courses for the Intermediate Degree of the BA (London, External). The house would soon be growing from a one-roof to a two-roof, perhaps even a three-roof and shed. Who knows, my stepfather could make corporal soon: lock-up and lick-up a couple of "bad men" and make sergeant.

Things were becoming respectable in the scheme of things. It would not be like the homes in Belleville but it would be clean enough for a stranger to enter and accept a glass of ice water in. It was to be my castle. And if my stepfather was liked and my industrious mother continued selling "a few things" through the kitchen window, then in good short time, who knows, we would have "water and 'lectricity running inside the house!" The future looked good. I could become a barrister: a legal fool!

I would take my stepfather's food in the three-tier carrier and linger about the court yard and dream of becoming a barrister and see and feel myself wearing the wig and two strips of white attached to the hard white collar. Every other boy at Combermere wanted to be a barrister-at-law. It seemed as if it was the only profession open to us. And it meant going *up* to England. Nothing could be better than seeing the Mother Country with your own eyes.

So the house was growing. Each time the man delivered four new boards, I saw my mother becoming prouder, more "pow'ful," telling the neighbours by gesture and by the antics of possession that she was somebody too. The "few things" sold through the kitchen window turned into black pudding and souce on Saturdays, and fish cakes during the week. She had a "part" in a pig; and a "part" in somebody's cow. We were gentlemen farmers. *Cutting and contriving*, my mother called it.

She worked hard. All women in those days worked hard.

My mother got up at five and cleaned the pots and pans from the previous night, and cooked a full meal before seven, on a stove made of three big rocks and fuelled by dried rotten sugar cane.

I went to the standpipe for water, filled three huge barrels

172

and placed the bleached flour bag over it "to keep out the blasted larvees," then my mother "went into the ground" to tie out the stocks, some of which we owned, some of which we had "parts" in. When I came back I bathed in the coldest water imaginable.

Dressed in my school uniform, I jumped on my bicycle and ticked all the way to 'Strict A or 'Strict B or 'Strict D, with the white enamel carrier of three tiers, each containing a different course of the meal for my stepfather. Sometimes my uniform would be soiled, through a careless rock in the road or a fowl or faulty brakes; and the sauce of the fried pork would splatter. I would ride all the way back to Flagstaff Road, chasing school buses and cars and other people on bicycles, to get my book bag in time to reach Combermere before nine o'clock.

There was no question now of showing hands and ears for inspection by the Major at the front gate. Cleanliness and godliness were left behind at St. Matthias. Some masters knew absolutely nothing and cared nothing about their students. Some did not know what life was like for these boys beyond the iron gate of Combermere.

In fits of temper and meanness, some masters would put us in detention for weeks. It could be because they had failed an exam taken by correspondence, had a quarrel with a wicked wife, a baby conceived by a woman they did not love.

Whenever I was put in detention, it meant that my mother had to walk to the various districts of the police sub-stations with my stepfather's food. She hated Combermere on these days and never let me forget it. "Cawmere mashing up my life, boy!"

The roads in Barbados were originally used by animals. They were built for animals. They are still like patterns in a spider's web. So the shortest road between the village and 'Strict D is not a straight line. You would have to ride or walk miles out of your way, along donkey-cart lanes, through cane-breks and fields, over hill and dale. But if you were a bird, you could fly the distance like a breeze.

THIRTY

When my stepfather was stationed at the Central Police
Station, it was fun. I was bigger and could request time for
myself from my mother — perhaps to visit the British Council,
sit and drink tea and pretend to be an Englishman; or to
listen to classical music with the Harrison College boys and
the Queen's College girls; or go to the public library to engage
in reading races with Kenny and another friend, Ralph Hare-
wood. But I would have to ask for this time with care. In her
eyes I was never too old for a flogging.

We were all three of us getting on in the world. New
arrangements had to be made for our lives. So we began to
send the food by bus. After school I would ride down to the
British Council and sit in a chair and read the pages of the
London Times or *The Listener*. But before I had finished
reading the magazine, I would be thinking of the carrier with
the food on the bus. The bus was not always dependable.

The carrier was put on the bus at Flagstaff Road at eight
in the morning or one in the afternoon. When the bus
reached Town, a woman or a man, paid by the policemen,
would take off the carrier and carry it, along with others in
his contract, to Central.

But sometimes they didn't. And the food would ride
again from Town to St. Patrick's and down again to Town.
The bus driver or the bus conductor might not have been
given his "piece o' change" to make him considerate, and

174

he would ignore the food. "Yuh don't play with a man's food!" But he would never allow anyone to touch the food.

Some carriers were dispatched by bus, and with a padlock and two keys: one kept by the policeman, the other by the wife or the "keep-miss." Some were padlocked and put in baskets which were themselves padlocked. "Yuh don't mek sport with a man's food!"

So the food might travel until it became porridge, if it was cou-cou; or pudding, if it was soup. When it was "dry food," boiled potatoes, boiled yams, boiled eddoes with a fish sauce, nothing happened except that it was really dry after the bouncing bus ride throughout the country.

Those policemen who hadn't given the conductor and the driver — necessary agents in this chain of couriers — a "piece o' change" had their food put under one of the seats at the back of the bus. Others who "handled them proper" and "as man" had their food placed under the watchful eye of the driver.

Sometimes there was trouble. Ants. Red ants. Brown ants. Black ants. Many times I would see a policeman at Central, with an enamel spoon, cursing as he tried to detect ant after ant from among the salt-fish sauce and the *bread-kind*. Some got away. But most perished for their stinging persistence in the bellies of the angry, hungry policemen.

The berries would fall on my head. Women who kept time around the law courts, and men who walked behind the barristers carrying their blue bags with gold tassels over their shoulders, men who succeeded in looking and behaving more important than the barristers themselves, were the pageantry of the court yard.

The women were sometimes called false oath-takers. Men

would be pleading their cases with the barristers. A child had to be supported. A woman was charging them with assault and battery. There was the possibility of being locked up.

"Skipper. Man, skipper, I depending on you, yuh!"

And the civil servants were walking sternly, their arms filled with big files containing dangerous information that could send a man to prison for life. These young men seemed to have forgotten their more meagre days at Combermere. They were the big men now. In collar and tie. These were the men who as boys had done well in the Senior Cambridge. Civil servants in Town: sanitary inspectors among the larvees, in the hidden country closets. And all of them thought of getting away, "leffing," going up to London to work on London Transport and punch tickets, and in the twinkling of an eye return as a barrister-at-law. They performed their duties with this thought at the back of their minds.

I can see Ranny Douglas, just back from London, tall and gaunt, his head bent to the ground because intelligent men are supposed to walk that way.

"Skipper, I dropping by your chambers, now-now-now!"

And I can see C. Henderson-Clarke, QC, a wisp of a man in stature, but an intellectual giant. Small and immaculate and smart, with his black robes askew to add to this brilliance. A real legal brain: a legal fool!

"Yer honner! Yer honner, I passing 'cross, for the little thing you promise, hear?"

And Grantley Adams, the man who was our leader. Black and with a smile on his bowed face, a smile which told he was not really smiling. Black, and an example of the heights we could reach. And if we did not take his example, we could always walk across to the House of Assembly and see the statue of Sir Conrad Reeves, the first black Chief Justice of Barbados, the son of a slave woman.

And the Lord Chief Justice, sombre in red or purple, and whiter white of wig, his spectacles falling off his nose, scratching noisily with a pen in the silent court; raising his nose every now and then to smell the truth in a word, to ask a

176

question, to say, "Objection overruled." Then to return to the scratching, without which you would have thought he was asleep up there on that formidable throne.

And Dipper Barrow, youngest in this firmament of legal stars, legal fools! We watched the barristers, and did not think of the doctors because they were not dramatic enough. We worshipped stars. And we worshipped style.

Behind and above the Lord Chief Justice was the insignia of the royal coat of arms, and the foreboding white sculpture of a woman dressed in a transparent robe like a nightgown. In one hand she held a pair of scales like the one Miss Bryan used in her shop; and in the other hand, a sword like the one the Governor carried in his white-sashed waist on the Queen's birthday on the Garrison Savannah.

The berries are falling on my head. A man comes out with two policemen walking beside him. The man does not look right and does not look left. His friends and family and his woman are in the crowd, and there are false oath-takers there too.

The young barristers-at-law — the "at law" part of their title attracted me most — are walking like penguins in black and little white, with the wig appearing heavier in the sun. They are wearing striped grey trousers and silk jackets, and oh my God, the starched white shirt and the two strips of white at the neck — all of this in a temperature of 105 degrees. You have to be bred in great houses, and in Humber-Hawkes, to wear this attire in sweltering heat and not sweat. To sweat means you do not belong to this aristocracy of inappropriate dress.

You can hear, if you are not dreaming, the footsteps of the defending and accusing men crushing the berries in their walk.

The people in the court yard move aside and the powerful walk through the silent aisle. The man who walks between the two policemen is handcuffed and ragged, barefooted and black; his shirt-tail is almost out of his trousers, and the cap on his head does not match his other garments.

The berries continue to fall on my head. I dream of walking

177

up the stone steps and entering the grand doors and bowing and saying, "Objection, muh Lud!" and bowing again.

"Skipper! Skipper!"

"Gorblummuh, he got to get off! He got to get off, once he have the great Henderson-Clarke. That man know law. The great Henderson-Clarke, QC, going get he off! And on the smallest point o' law!"

"Aw right, Skipper! How the mistress? Aw right! I bringing down a couple breadfruits from the land for you. Heh-heh-heh! Aw right! . . . That is man! That is a giant when yuh come to law and torts and contracks!"

"O-yez, o-yez, o-yez, all you gathered in this honourable court, please rise. . ."

The man with the two policemen at his side, manacled to them, to their black sides, walks in and all is lost. . . The doors are closed and I have to get the three-tier carrier and return to Flagstaff Road before it is too late to ride through Belleville Avenue.

The berries still fall. And whenever I get a chance, I mash them with my shoes. And always they make a slight protest.

Law is on my mind. And I pattern myself after the great C. Henderson-Clarke, QC, and learn which Inn of Court he attended; because if it is the Middle Temple, then the Middle Temple is the place which produces the best barristers-at-law, these legal fools.

I return to Flagstaff Road after these dreams in the gathering dusk and repeat all the morning chores in reverse order. I settle down in front of the kerosene lamp with the home-made brown paper shade, and spend the long mosquitoed night dreaming of London, of wigs and black robes and the Middle Temple.

My mother interrupts. "Don't forget to get up early and carry the sheeps up in the ground!"

I leave England and temples and suddenly I see a cockroach fluttering his way back to the toilet pit.

THIRTY-ONE

"I am going to Amurca after I sit this examination, to enter Columbia University."

"My father get me a job in the Civil Service. In the Colonial Secretary's Office."

"I am going to be a teacher. Elementary school."

"If I pass, I am going to be working for my uncle, as a' overseer. If I fail, whiching is the way I had better see this thing, because I can't make head nor tail o' this blasted Latin, then I am going to be a sanitary inspector. Be-Jesus Christ, when you fellows having a good time in the Civil Service or in Amurca, I am going to be looking for larvees!"

"I don't know yet what I am going to do, or what I am going to be."

"The headmaster say he is going to write me a testimonial to help me to get in the Civil Service."

"My uncle the solicitor getting me artickled."

"If I pass in Latin, and that is a big if, and if I get through mathematics, I think I'll be getting a job at Weatherhead's, the druggists in Town. As an apprentice druggist."

"Everybody saying what they are going to be, except you, Tom. What you going to be?"

"My aunt in Panama sending me to Harsun College. . . ."

"If yuh pass!"

"If I pass."

"Do you want to hear something? All these years we

going to Cawmere, and right over there, with a wire fence dividing we, is Harsun College. And you want to know something? None o' we never even as much as bend down and go under the wire and walk through Harsun College. Who here has ever walked through Harsun College grounds? You see what I mean? That is a different world! A different world they have over there. And now my boy going over there! In a different world."

"I hear that the work over there at Harrison is real hard. I hear too that the masters over there real cruel. I hear that there's a lotta fellows going to Harrison College who does go mad, because of the amount of work they have to study. I hear that for one night of homework they set a hundred lines o' Latin, a hundred lines o' Greek, five chapters o' Ancient History, five chapters o' Greek history, a distinction Latin prose, a distinction Greek prose, a pass Latin prose, and a pass Greek prose, plus Unseens, plus Shakespeare, Milton, Chaucer, Ben Johnson. . . I hear from a fellow who goes to Harrison College that they. . . "

The fifth formers could take time off from the regular schedule of classes to prepare for the examination. The Cambridge University Senior Cambridge Examination (Overseas). We were overseas people. Some of the banks in our country said they were overseas banks too. Long-distance calls were called overseas calls. Barclay's was Barclay's, Dominion, Colonial and Overseas. We had got to know our place as overseas people.

The Cambridge examinations were set by some learned professors who lived in England, more learned than anybody in Barbados. They were sent down to Barbados by English post, and were kept sealed somewhere in the Ministry of

180

Education until that frightening day when they were opened with great caution, determination and fuss.

We would write these Cambridge examinations; and our answers would be sent back up to England, to those same learned professors, who must have marvelled at the answers we gave them to these overseas questions, questions which had nothing to do with the way we lived, with the way we understood ourselves, with the way we saw ourselves. But they were "educated" questions, and we were educated Combermere boys.

So we prepared ourselves for this overseas examination, the most important event in our lives. It could determine whether we were going to be sanitary inspectors for the rest of our lives or were going to get into the Civil Service, not the Department of Customs, which buried men alive from drink, but the "Col-Sec's Office," and rise to positions of power and hold confidential files under the soiled arms of our white shirts. Perhaps to be given an OBE at age fifty, with one foot in the grave.

It determined whether we were going to languish and starve on small salaries as elementary school teachers, and take out our anger and disappointment on the small frightened boys in those dark, steamy and under-equipped school rooms; and get a pension.

It determined whether we were going to be among the lucky clear-skinned few who would spend the rest of their lives riding on the back of a brown horse in the broiling hot sun, with a white cork hat; riding through the tall green canes, tall enough to hide the occasional orgasm through the mercy of some field woman who had to give up her body in order to keep her job and feed her children, the brightest of whom might be at this same Combermere School; and get a pick on the Barbados Polo Team.

This examination determined whether we would qualify and go up to England by boat, third class, tourist class, with a borrowed winter coat, and enter one of the Inns of Court, and after eighteen months' studying the law, return and flood the country; and get MP behind our name.

It determined whether we would be able to enter a British university.

It meant life and could mean death. If you were not lucky and careful and had failed, it meant that for generations afterwards people would whisper when you passed, and say that you had wasted your mother's money and had not got your Senior Cambridge.

And because it meant all of this, we buckled ourselves down in strange and superstitious ways in order to pass this examination. The pass word was study: study hard. Beat your brains out.

We sucked raw eggs to fertilize the brain, to sharpen the retentive capacities. Everything had to be learned by heart. Some of us starved ourselves because superstition told us that to be intelligent, to be a learning fool, you couldn't eat the heavy food, "dry food," boiled yams, potatoes, eddoes and hard dumplings, which we had been eating all our lives.

We drank Guinness, unmindful at this precarious time of the dangers in the Guinness of multiplying our young unused sperms and making us breed women. But we were at the climax of our education. Soon we would be fathering children. So the Guinness with the raw egg beaten up in it, with a shot of dark rum and some nutmeg, the identical training tonic of my running days, was no real danger now. We would soon be working men. Maho—d

The Major, still without his pips of Colonial Service in the British Army, stopped calling us boys and called us men. It frightened some of us. To be a man in the village, a different world from Combermere, different like the world of Harrison College is different, to be a man meant you had children, a job, could afford child-money if you had the misfortune to breed a woman, and admitted to the error of lust and pleasure but did not marry the unfortunate girl. The courts, with the berries dropping on your head, saw to that: "Would you de-flower this poor but decent girl and then say that you not supporting her offspring? Wha'?"

Some of us climbed trees and built seats in them, escaping from the lesser mortals of mother and father, brothers and sisters who were not at high school. And we crammed our heads with Pythagoras Theorem, with the *Axe of the 'Postles*, with French, with Latin, and of course with irregular verbs.

We remained in the trees until the black birds came and reminded us that trees are for the birds. And we climbed down with our old, torn, first-edition texts of this strange and important knowledge which a learned professor up in England would try to unravel, and then pass or fail us.

But for the time being we wore our horn-rimmed spectacles not because our eyes were weak but because the Cawmere boy had to wear glasses, to look like a student.

We walked through the lanes and mashed cow dung with our bare feet; we crushed centipedes, living and dead. We were reprieved from carrying the three-tier white enamel carrier with the policeman's lunch and dinner, and from doing all of the chores around the house, because our mothers knew that the examination was important.

A mother would hang her head in sorrow, be disgraced, if her son had thrown all her money "in Maxwell's Pond" and had failed. To fail meant you had put back the clock. You would be a sanitary inspector for the rest of your days, and commune with faeces and larvees.

So we walked from the trees or from our fathers' "studies" or from the cow pen when the cow was tied out in the ground, or from a friend's verandah, and we kept our heads buried in the intractable ground, seeing in the shapeless patterns of the land the answers to the questions which were set in the examination in England but which would determine our lives in Barbados.

But Barbados was known as Little England. There was not much that was irrelevant about the arrangement.

Some of us sat up all night, trying to remember in one week what had been impossible to learn in one year. And when we moved from the bad light of the kerosene lamp, we had headaches. But it was status to have a headache.

183

Anyone who did not study "hard things," who had not read Latin, could not have a headache.

So we told our mothers we had "bad bad headaches," and our mothers broadcast the problem throughout the village, and everybody came to their rescue. Fresh limes were cut in half and the juice squeezed and rubbed around the forehead, and some of them sucked. Limacol and Bay rum were brought from the shop on trust, no mention being made now of payment. And these were rubbed around our necks and foreheads. The best parts of the chicken, the best parts of the pork chop, with the skin on it, the best chicken soup, were set aside for the Senior Cambridge boy. Wincarnis wine, vitamins, iron drops and iron tablets were got from the drug store out the front road, or from Knight's or Weatherhead's on Broad Street in Town, "because this boy-child o' mine have a headache and I have to get everything to make him pass this examination."

And then the day came.

We wore our best clothes, as if we were going to a wedding. Our best clothes, clothes which we had worn the previous Christmas or Easter, came out at this examination. For the first time we got a picture of the meanness of the tailors in the various villages of the island; of the needleworkers; and sometimes of the shoemakers, for this was still a time when a shoemaker made a shoe.

We saw that the Indian man had traversed the entire island, for here before our eyes on this terrible first day of the Senior Cambridge Examination we saw all kinds of silk shirts, made by all kinds of hands.

Soon after arrival, the first traces of tension and fear marked their fingers with indelible perspiration stains. The colours of the shirts changed immediately around the under arms.

Shoes were shiny and creaking, and some had to be taken off because they were not bought for walking but for showing the neighbour that your boy had proper shoes. And these shoes, which would never fit the foot again, had to be worn around the neck: tied by their laces.

Heads with new haircuts made it difficult to recognize close friends, because the neighbourhood barbers had perhaps begun their tasks too late under the tree in the back yard, and the failing light had caused the hand with the glass-bottle blade to slip and falter, cutting more hair than was needed.

Unopened bottles of Quink ink were bravely displayed. New pens would leak in nervous hands, and nibs break off.

On this morning you got twice the amount of lunch money that you got for a whole week. If the belly was not full, you could not concentrate on these difficult overseas examination questions.

Some of us fainted from the heat and from fear. We all understood what the morning stood for. And when the bell rang and we were ushered by name into the hall and told to sit in alphabetical order, we were relieved. Now it was too late. It meant that all the formulas we had written on our shirt cuffs, or in our palms, or in our minds, would either evaporate in the perspiration of tension or disappear because we were scared.

The room is quiet. You look around at your friend, at the brightest boy in the class, at the dumbest boy in the school, and you wonder how they will make out. And you look around again and realize that you are isolated on this crucial day when you may need help most; and the boy in your class for a whole year who would lend you a helping hand with the conjugation of an irregular verb is now, alas, far, far from you because of a simple thing like the letter of his surname.

You are near the front, near the invigilator, usually a priest whom you have never seen before and will never see again; and you know he will give you no chance. You cannot wander with your eyes in strained concentration onto another boy's examination book. This priest will not give you a break, even if he only feels you are cheating.

Papers are taken out of the large brown envelopes with On Her Majesty's Service printed on them. The invigilator's hands are trembling. He knows the importance of these examinations, of the great trust which the overseas professors and the government of this overseered country have placed in his hands. He had already passed this route. He is a member of the Anglican Church, and he is at least a Bachelor of Theology.

He looks at the examination papers, one for each boy, and his mind must go back to those days, long ago in time but not in history, when he sat in a room like this, facing the Senior Cambridge Overseas Examination. You cannot expect softness from him, for the island is one school of crabs in fierce competition. Perhaps this priest's marks are still unsurpassed. They are certainly written down somewhere in the ministry; and he will not bless you for reaching his grade!

You glance again for the last time at the brightest boy, at the dumbest boy, at your friend, in case one is not the other, and you feel a nausea in your stomach. One or two boys are excused, and they run from the room holding their mouths. They have gone to vomit.

And suddenly you are alone. You are in a cell. It is cold and humid at the same time. Your whole life comes before you, and you cannot do very much about it.

"A fellow who knew that the Scripture exam was going be on the Monday after the first week o' the Senior Cambridge went home on the Friday and read up the commentary by Reverend Stanley on the Feeding of the Five Thousand. And

he write out the whole commentary word for word. Because he did know that in twenty consecutive examinations the Cambridge people had ask the same question 'bout the Feeding of the Five Thousand.

"He came back to the exam room on the Monday morning smiling. Bram! First question on the paper, 'Explain the Feeding of the Five Thousand.' All during the exam, people sweating, people looking left and right trying to pick a message in Morse code outta a fellow's eyes, people scratching their heads, the blasted questions so hard. And this fellow relaxing and playing real cool.

"When the bell ring and the invigilator came round to pick up the papers, this fellow who had stole a' examination book the Friday before just write his name on the book with the commentary he had copied from Reverend Stanley, and his examination number, and gave it in.

"Boy, when you hear the shout, a big noise up in the Overseas office in Cambridge, in England. Yuh see, the fellow had use blue Quink ink at home writing out the commentary, and on this Monday he forget and use black Quink ink to write his name and number. And they put the two inks under periscopes and other things, took fingerprints and so on.

"Well, you can imagine what happened after that. One answer he write in blue Quink ink, and the other three in black Quink ink! They failed him in every blasted subject, although he had get distinctions in three others. Today if you go down Broad Street, you would see 'Black-and-Blue' walking 'bout selling life insurance. . . . "

THIRTY-TWO

Time became heavy and long. The Senior Cambridge men had to wait for the results until September, before they could get the jobs they were promised. Some would wait longer. Those who had failed would never get jobs. Some went to Amurca, to uncles and aunts. Kenny was one of them. Some became policemen. Some just disappeared.

Those of us who were in the Cadet Corps had a reprieve from this languorous time. There was a camp for all the cadets in the country. Harrison College would be there. The Lodge School would be there. And Combermere.

I was now sergeant-major, the highest-ranking boy at Combermere; the highest rank a boy could hold.

The camp was like a mock army. In a mock war. Doing mock things. For the first time for the Combermere Army, we held guns with pins which fired real bullets or blanks. We were put on a firing range for the first time, and told to "shoot." Some of us wet our pants. And when they put grenades into our hands and told us to count to five and throw them into the sea because they were the real things, we panicked and counted only to three and threw them just three yards below our feet, and we all had to dive and eat the sand. But no one killed himself.

The food was good. For many of us, it was the best food we had ever eaten. We put on weight. We were relaxed in this mock sport of war. We were breathing in the fresh country air of Walkers, and considered making a career out of the Army, an aspiration based on the quality and quantity of the food. And we thought of Sleepy, who had passed this march before.

I was going to be at Harrison College the next term, in September. Even before this camp, I knew that none of the present second or first lieutenants would be returning to Harrison College. So I, one of the senior cadets in the island, was sure to get a commission. From sergeant-major at Combermere to second lieutenant at Harrison College.

I spent most of my time thinking of Sleepy. I polished my imitation of his walk, cockier now, and could see the pips on my shoulder. I thought of the Major and never understood why he did not get a kick out of wearing his own pips. Did "demobilization" mean "dismissal"?

I thought of the scores of chickens and pullets in our back yard in Flagstaff Road, and how I had picked off their pips from their tongues by using ashes and oil.

We "invaded" the village of Walkers many times; marched through the streets singing *John Brown's Body* all this long way from Tipperary. It was hip and pip and hooray! We glanced at girls in the village and made dates with them, but they could not hear because we were moving now, we were in the Army!

And then one night after lights out, the sergeant-major from the Lodge School and I went down the sand dune of a hill from the camp, to Walkers village. We were away from the alarum and parades of spit and polish, the saluting of boy officers from Harrison College and officers from the Barbados Regiment who were teaching us how to be real like they were.

That night the Harrison College army were doing guard duty. But my friend had seen a girl from the village and he wanted her to fall in love with him, to see her for the last time and kiss her before we broke camp at nine o'clock the next morning. And as one soldier to another, I kept him company.

It was a soft time of fun and talking under the young

189

lady's window, because we were not permitted to enter her parents' drawing room; for this relationship was the relationship of a soldier and a village girl, and it had not even passed the stage of informality.

My friend wore the topee perhaps to impress the girl. We used to buckle our topees under our chins at night, to make us look like fighter pilots. He carried the flashlight he had brought to the camp two weeks before. The batteries were almost dead now.

He had his fill of talk, with confessions and promises of love. He held the girl's hand for one moment in the dark night, then we set off back up the hill.

"I going to Codrington College next week to study theology and ethics," he said. "Perhaps, might even continue with the army."

And then misfortune befell us. He dropped his topee among the brush and bush and sand of the hill; and because the flashlight was too weak, we could not find it. Hours passed.

"Man, I need it for the parade tomorrow," he said. "How would it look for a sergeant-major to be on parade, and the last one at that, without a hat?"

Eventually we found the topee. And we scrambled up the hill, quiet as spies, fierce as desperadoes, tense as guerrillas. And when we stopped just outside the fence of the camp and got ready to bound in the direction of our tents, the voice assaulted us.

"Halt! Who goes there — friend or foe?" This sounded like real war. "Advance and be recognized!"

We were jolted from this mock camp into a cold and brutal danger of what it meant to be in a mock army with "soldiers" from Harrison College who imagined they were in the British Army. A sergeant-major from Combermere School and a sergeant-major from the Lodge School, both of us on the pinnacle of a commission.

It became cold. My fist was ready. It meant knocking this fat young mock sentry from Harrison College out cold, or

190

else confronting recognition and the loss of face. But they were ready for us. Ready for me. Spies had been planted. Mock spies.

We were "arrested" and marched off to the guard tent, and awakened each time the mock guards changed, and given coffee to keep us awake and restless throughout the long cold night. Before dawn came, news had spread throughout the camp like an epidemic.

"They catch the Cawmere sar-major sneaking out! They going court-martial he first thing in the morning!"

All of a sudden I felt that there had never been anything mock about this camp; that everything had been real beneath the camouflage and the sport; that cadets and soldiers had been thinking seriously about my military career while I was bathing in the sport of the board guns and mock drills and giving orders.

The morning broke. There was a bright sun. There were birds. There was spit and polish. The breeze from the sea at Walkers was cool. There was joy all around me. But the morning was sad.

They formed in ranks, according to school, stiff and erect. No man smiling, no man doubting the sombre moment. They looked straight ahead, perhaps at nothing but their dreams and expectations, as they were taught to do when at attention. They formed around me, "the Cawmere sar-major," and around my friend, topeed and sad.

I was thinking of Amurca, of those men who had left during the war years, to get away from the stiff conduct and class regimentation. Of those men who had died in the war: on land, on sea, and in the air. I was thinking of those boys who had failed their Senior Cambridge Examination, who were somewhere else on this small island of a country, remembering the Latin and the irregular verbs, but not enough to guarantee a job in the Civil Service in the "Col-Sec's Office"!

I was far from the moment of military precision when the officer — I cannot remember whether he was the colonel of the Regiment or the captain of our own Cadet Corps — touched the three stripes with the Imperial Crown on my shoulders and for a fleeting moment looked into my eyes. And I saw in his eyes regret, perhaps disbelief, hurt and anger, because I had let him down.

He touched the stripes, then tightened his grip and ripped the rank from my shoulders.

I knew then that the time had come for me to dream of a new beginning. I remember nothing after that. I do not remember one detail of the breaking of camp, nothing about the drive back to Combermere in the Regiment's lorries, and then the journey to my home where the food would be so different from this two-week picnic. I remember nothing. And I will remember nothing more.

And even when I entered Harrison College the next term and saw my rank posted on the notice board beside the clock tower outside the classical sixth form — A. A. C. Clarke: Acting Lance Corporal — I thought only of Sleepy Smith and his sombre voice in the translation of Vergil, *The Aeneid*, Book One: *"I sing of arms and a hero, who first sailed from the shores of Troy. . . "*

The year was one thousand, nine hundred and fifty.